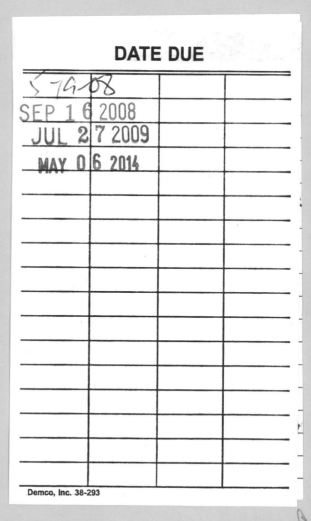

BLACK, WHITE, AND JEWISH

BLACK, WHITE, AND JEWISH

*Autobiography of
a Shifting Self*

REBECCA WALKER

RIVERHEAD BOOKS
a member of Penguin Putnam Inc.
NEW YORK
2001

RIVERHEAD BOOKS
a member of
Penguin Putnam Inc.
375 Hudson Street
New York, NY 10014

Library of Congress Cataloging-in-Publication Data

Walker, Rebecca.
    Black, white, and Jewish : autobiography of a shifting self /
by Rebecca Walker.
        p.   cm.
    ISBN 1-57322-169-4
        1. Walker, Rebecca.   2. Racially mixed people—
United States—Race identity.   3. Racially mixed people—United
States—Biography.   4. Daughters—United States—Biography.
5. Afro-American women—Biography.   6. Jewish women—
United States—Biography.   7. Walker, Alice, date.—Family.
I. Title.
    E184.A1.W214   2001   00-035292
    973.04'96073'0092—dc21
    [B]
Printed in the United States of America

10   9   8   7   6   5   4   3   2   1

This book is printed on acid-free paper. ∞

Book design by Marysarah Quinn

For my parents

BLACK, WHITE, AND JEWISH

I remember airports I remember air

I don't remember things. Like the names of streets and avenues I have driven down a hundred times, like the stories behind Jewish holidays I have celebrated since I was eleven, like the date of my father's birthday. At a funeral for a favorite uncle, I do not remember the names of cousins I played with as a child. For a few minutes, I do not remember the name of my dead uncle's wife. On her porch I stand blankly between her outstretched arms, my head spinning, suddenly unsure even of the ground upon which I stand. Who am I and why am I here? I cannot remember how we all are related.

There are thousands of large and small omissions, bits of information I swear normal people have built into their DNA: the speed of light, so-and-so's running mate twelve years ago, the capital of Wyoming, the way Treasury bills work. Mostly, I'm not bothered by my mind's resistance to what it considers meaningless, but sometimes I feel oddly off balance, like the whole world has figured out how to cope, how to master life on the grid, but me. Without a memory that invests in information retention, without a memory that can remind me at all times of who I definitively am, I feel amorphous, missing the unbroken black outline around my body that everyone else seems to have.

A good friend has decided that Soul is Mind, that Mind describes and encompasses the larger idea of Spirit. "You cannot Be without Mind," she says, referring to something which includes, but is much larger than, her brain. Knowing well the limitations of my own mind, I am skeptical, disapproving. "It's the heart," I say, laying my flat palm over my beating organ, feeling the heat grow between skin and skin, through the cotton of my tee shirt. "You cannot have Soul without heart." I, too, am referring to something ineffable, something much larger than the muscle in my chest.

We are talking about God, I think, and memory.

She shakes her head no as I look at her, wanting to remember how she looks to me on this Sunday afternoon in my living room with the sun streaming through the big old windows. My mind ticks away, registering her waffled army-green tee shirt, thick silver hoops, and brown, almond-shaped eyes. I sum her up, compare her today with her another day, piece her psyche together from all the strands of her childhood that I know. My eyes do all they can and then, as if considering a collage by Bearden or a painting by van Gogh, push the task gratefully onto my dumb, mute heart.

Because when it comes time to remember this woman it will not be all perfectly articulated platitudes or carefully constructed diagnoses. When it is time to remember her after she leaves it will be my heart—lazy, slow, decidedly not smart—that will pull and yearn and twist around like a dog in dirt. It will be my heart that will force my mind to remember her face, the way she felt lying next to me in the dark, the way she looked sitting on the sofa, telling me that Mind, to her, is everything. My heart will have registered the deeper meaning snaking and elusive beneath her disparate pieces; my heart alone will allow me to remember her whole.

I remember airports. The new one with the stained-glass-windowed, art-deco waiting room in Rochester, the one with tinted light blue glass and a super-efficient McDonald's in Manchester, Pittsburgh's airport-cum-shopping center: the Sky Mall. I remember Chicago's hyper-industrial steel-and-glass-corridored O'Hare, the pink and yellow neo-Aztec pyramid in Puerto Vallarta, the hazy, dirty carpeted halls and frenzied, wind-whipped baggage claim at LAX. I remember the SkyTel Pager booth at Atlanta International, the women in black sitting on the periphery of the giant flattened rectangle of Cairo's concrete Bedouin tent. I remember the bougainvillea bushes spilling out from clay pots at Nairobi, the Italian Modern with portholes in Milan, and the hushed, airy cathedral of blond wood and brushed aluminum in Hamburg.

I am more comfortable in airports than I am in either of the houses I call, with undeserved nostalgia, Home. I am more comfortable in airports than I was in any of the eight different schools where I learned all of the things I now cannot remember. Airports are limbo spaces—blank, undemanding, neutral. Expectations are clear. I am the passenger. I am coming or going. I am late, on time, or early. I must have a ticket. I must have identification. I must not carry a weapon. Beyond these qualifications, I do not have to define this body. I do not have to belong to one camp, school, or race, one fixed set of qualifiers, adjectives based on someone else's experience. I do not have to remember who I, or anyone else, thinks I am. I am transitional space, form-shifting space, place of a thousand hellos and a million goodbyes.

Another friend tells me hyperbolically that she enjoyed a six-month stay in jail, and that on some days she comes dizzying close to checking herself into the asylum. "I need to be confined," she says, and I know what she means. There is safety in four walls, in rituals boiled down into rules. Freedom can feel overwhelming. I would not trade it, but sometimes I want to be told what to do. I want to know constraints, boundaries. I want to know the limits of who I am. Tell me what I cannot do. Let me master myself within articulated limitations. Without these, I feel vast, out of control. Like I can too easily slip outside of my own life and into someone else's. Like if I am not careful, I could, as my friend who liked jail wishes to do often, close my eyes and disappear.

Growing up I did not, ever, feel contained. I never felt the four walls of my room or my apartment or my house or my town or my culture close around me; I never knew the feeling of the extended womb. My parents did not hold me tight, but encouraged me to go. They did not buffer, protect, watch out for, or look after me. I was watered, fed, admired, stroked, and expected to grow. I was mostly left alone to discover the world and my place in it. From the houses and apartments in which I lived, I remember most of all the doors and how they opened for me. I remember the windows and how I never looked out of them longingly, for outside was never kept from me. I remember coming and going, going and coming. That, for me, was home.

I am not tragic I am no

START

On my first birthday I am given my favorite foods: chitterlings and chocolate cake. Daddy goes to Estelle's, the soul food place on the other side of town where he is the only white customer, and brings me home a large order of the pig intestines. Mama puts me in my big wooden high chair with the smooth curved piping, and then feeds me one slimy pale gray glob after another while Daddy sits at the table, grinning.

After I have eaten all of the chitterlings, Mama has to peel my tiny fingers from the container to make me let it go. Then she sets a chocolate cake with a big number one candle sticking up from the middle down in front of me, singing "Happy Birthday" softly, so that only I can hear. For a few seconds Mama and Daddy wait, expectant and wide-eyed, to see what I'll do. I giggle, squeal, look at them, and then dig into the cake with my bare hands, smearing the sticky sweetness all over my face and pushing what's left into my mouth. I rub cake in my hair, over my eyes. I slap my hands on the high chair, putting some cake on it, too.

My parents laugh out loud for a few seconds; then my father wraps his arm around my mother's waist, patting her hip with a cupped hand. For a few seconds we are frozen in time. Then my father pushes his chair out from the table, cuts himself a piece of the chocolate cake, and goes to work.

Y ou may want to ask about the story of your birth, and I mean down to the tiniest details. Were you born during the biggest snowstorm your town had seen in fifty years? Did your father stop at the liquor store on the way to the hospital? Did you refuse to appear, holding on to the inside of your mother's womb for days? Some sinewy thread of meaning is in there somewhere, putting a new spin on the now utterly simplistic nature-nurture debate. Your job is to listen carefully and let your imagination reconstruct the narrative, pausing on hot spots like hands over a Ouija board.

I was born in November 1969, in Jackson, Mississippi, seventeen months after Dr. King was shot. When my mother went into labor my father was in New Orleans arguing a case on behalf of black people who didn't have streetlights or sewage systems in their neighborhoods. Daddy told the judge that his wife was in labor, turned his case over to co-counsel, and caught the last plane back to Jackson.

When I picture him, I conjure a civil rights Superman flying through a snowstorm in gray polyester pants and a white shirt, a dirty beige suede Wallabee touching down on the curb outside our house in the first black middle-class subdivision in Jackson. He bounds to the door, gallantly gathers up my very pregnant mother who has been waiting, resplendent in her African muumuu, and whisks her to the newly desegregated hospital. For this final leg, he drives a huge, hopelessly American Oldsmobile Toronado.

Mama remembers long lines of waiting black women at this hospital, screaming in the hallways, each encased in her own private hell. Daddy remembers that I was born with my eyes open, that I smiled when I saw him, a look of recognition piercing the air between us like lightning.

And then, on my twenty-fifth birthday, Daddy remembers something I've not heard before: A nurse walks into Mama's room, my birth certificate in hand. At first glance, all of the information seems straightforward enough: mother, father, address, and so on. But next to boxes labeled "Mother's Race" and "Father's Race," which read Negro and Caucasian, there is a curious note tucked into the margin. "Correct?" it says. "Correct?" a faceless questioner wants to know. Is this union, this marriage, and especially this offspring, correct?

A mulatta baby swaddled and held in loving arms, two brown, two white, in the middle of the segregated South. I'm sure the nurses didn't have many reference points. Let's see. Black. White. Nigger. Jew. That makes me the tragic mulatta caught between both worlds like the proverbial deer in the headlights. I am Mammy's near-white little girl who plunges to her death, screaming, "I don't want to be colored, I don't want to be like you!" in the film classic *Imitation of Life*. I'm the one in the Langston Hughes poem with the white daddy and the black mama who doesn't know where she'll rest her head when she's dead: the colored buryin' ground behind the chapel or the white man's cemetery behind gates on the hill.

But maybe I'm being melodramatic. Even though I am surely one of the first interracial babies this hospital has ever seen, maybe the nurses take a liking to my parents, noting with recognition their ineffable humanness: Daddy with his bunch of red roses and queasiness at the sight of blood, Mama with her stoic, silent pain. Maybe the nurses don't load my future up with tired, just-off-the-plantation narratives. Perhaps they don't give it a second thought. Following standard procedure, they wash my mother's blood off my newborn body, cut our fleshy cord, and lay me gently over Mama's thumping heart. *Place infant face down on mother's left breast, check blankets, turn, walk out of room, close door, walk up hallway,* and so on. Could I be just another child stepping out into some unknown destiny?

JACKSON

My cousin Linda comes from Boston to help take care of me while my mother writes and my father works at the office. Linda has bright red hair and reddish brown skin to match. Linda sits on our tiny porch for hours, in the same chair Daddy sits in sometimes with the rifle and the dog, waiting for the Klan to come. Linda sits there and watches the cars go by. When she sees the one she wants, she stands up and points. She says she wants a black Mustang, rag top. "That car is live," I say, putting extra emphasis on *live* but not sounding quite as smooth as my cousin. "Rag top," I say, trying it on as we sit together on the cement porch.

Linda gets sick after a few weeks and can't get out of the extra bed in my room. She tells me secretly, late at night from underneath all our extra quilts and afghans, that she wants to stay here with us forever, that she loves Uncle Mel, wants to marry Uncle Mel. She says, "Your daddy is a good white man!" and smiles, her big teeth all white and perfect.

Linda is sick for a long time. Does she have the mumps, tonsillitis? Daddy says it's because she doesn't want to go home. Mama ends up taking care of both of us. She boils water in the yellow kettle and makes Linda honey and lemon tea, Mama's cold specialty. She tells me and Linda to lie on the brown sofa in the living room, in the sun. Linda lies one way on the corduroy couch, I the other. Before she goes back into her study, Mama covers us with the big, colorful afghan.

Linda and I stay there, whispering, and tickling each other with our toes until it is dark, listening to the click-clacking of Mama's typewriter, until we see the shadowy outline of Daddy walk through the front door.

Mrs. Dixon comes twice a month to vacuum our house and clean the kitchen and bathroom. She is tall and light-skinned and wears her hair pulled back in a bun. She is older than Mama, and very quiet. I know she is in the house only because of the sound of the vacuum cleaner, which seems especially loud in our house that is usually so still and silent.

Sometimes, after Mrs. Dixon goes home and leaves the house with a clean lemony smell, Mama puts on a Roberta Flack or Al Green record and runs a bath for us. After we scrub and wash with Tone soap or Dial, we spread our bright orange towels out in the warm patches of sunlight that streak the light wood of the living-room floor. We rub cocoa butter lotion all over our bodies and then do our exercises, leg lifts, until our legs hurt and we can't do any more. Sometimes we fall asleep there, after the arm on the phonograph swings itself back into place, my little copper form pressed against the smooth warm length of my mother's cherry-brown body.

Grandma Miriam comes for a visit. She says she can't stay away from her first-born, oldest grandchild. She drives up in her yellow Plymouth Gran Fury and right away starts talking about all the things we don't have and what is wrong with our house. She buys Mama a washer-dryer in one and a sewing machine. She buys me a Mickey Mouse watch that doesn't stay on my wrist. It is way too big, but she says I will grow into it. She also buys me a package of pens with my name printed on them in gold.

Grandma Miriam is so strong, sometimes when she picks me up it hurts, holding too tight when I want to get down. She also walks fast. She also always turns up our air conditioner because she says it is too hot "down here." She lives in Brooklyn, the place where Daddy was born. She brought all of her clothes and presents and everything in a round red "valise" with a zipper opening and a loop for a handle. She has white skin and wears red lipstick and tells me that the nose she has now is not her real nose. When I ask her where her real nose is, she tells me, "Broken," and then right away starts talking about something else, like the heat.

Daddy seems happy Grandma came to see us, but Mama seems nervous, angry. I think this is because Grandma doesn't look at Mama. When she talks to Mama, she looks at me.

. . .

Mama has to have an operation on her eye. She leaves early one morning and doesn't come home until late the next day. I wait, listening all afternoon for her key in the lock. When the door finally swings open and I see the sleeve of her dark blue winter coat, my heart jumps. I want to run into her arms, but something stops me. Mama has a big white patch over her eye. She looks different, like the side of her body with the patch is lost, not there, or in the dark. Suddenly I am afraid that if I am not gentle, I will knock her down.

I must look worried because she smiles her big smile and tells me that she's all right. The operation wasn't as bad as she thought it would be.

I almost believe her.

Later, as she dresses to go out, Mama opens her straw jewelry basket and searches for a necklace to wear. I watch her, face resting in my upturned hands, as she tries first the heavy Indian silver amulet and then a simple stone on a leather strap. I notice that she holds her head a new way, hurt eye away from the mirror and chin slightly down.

After choosing not to wear either, she turns and kisses my forehead. Looking deep into my eyes she tells me that one day, all of the jewelry in the basket will belong to me.

Almost every week people come to our house to visit. They come from up north, they come from other countries. They come to see us, to see how we are living in Jackson. Most people bring presents for Mama: books, teas, quilts, bright-colored molas from Central America she puts on the walls. When my cousin Brenda comes, she brings presents for me. She brings soaps shaped like animals, puzzles with animals in them, books about animals, and my favorite, sheets with animals crowded onto them in orange, red, and purple packs.

Late at night between my jungle sheets, I imagine I am riding on the backs of giraffes and elephants, I imagine I can hear the sounds of the wild, of all the animals in the forest talking to one another like I have seen on my favorite television show, *Big Blue Marble*. When Mama comes in to check to see if I am asleep, I am not, but I shut my eyes tight and pretend that I am so that I can stay in the dark dark forest where it is moist and green, where I am surrounded by all my friends from the jungle.

Three days a week I go to Mrs. Cornelius's house for nursery school. Most often Daddy drops me off on his way to the office, or sometimes Mama will take me up the street, or Mrs. Cornelius will send her daughter Gloria to pick me up. Mrs. Cornelius's school is in her basement, which she has renovated with bright fluorescent lights, stick-down squares of yellow and white linoleum, and fake dark wood paneling.

Every day at lunchtime at Mrs. Cornelius's, we eat the same foods: black-eyed peas, collard greens, and sweet potatoes. I start to hate black-eyed peas from having them so often, but I love Mrs. Cornelius. She is like Grandma, only warmer, softer, and brown. She always pays special attention to me. On picture day she combs my hair, smoothing it away from my face. She says that I am pretty, and that even though I am the youngest at her school, I am the smartest. In the class picture, mine is the lightest face.

One day Daddy holds my hand as we cross the street in front of our house like usual, on our way to school. I am wearing my favorite orange and red striped Healthtex shirt and matching red pants with snaps up one leg. Suddenly Daddy stops and points in the direction of Mrs. Cornelius's house. He looks at me: "Do you think you can walk by yourself?"

With my eyes I find Mama, who waves and smiles encouragingly from the porch. "Don't worry, I'll watch you from here," Daddy says, but I'm already confused. He pats my backside. "Go on. Go to Mrs. Cornelius's house." I feel trapped, uncertain, and so I just stand there, looking first at Daddy and then across the street at Mama. Before I can say anything, Daddy nudges me again and I take a tentative step toward Mrs. Cornelius's house, my shoes tiny and white against the dirty gray pavement.

One night after I am supposed to be in bed, I crawl into Mama and Daddy's room, making my way around their big bed where they lie talking and reading the newspaper. Johnny Carson is on the television, and every few minutes Mama laughs, throwing her head back. From where I sit, underneath the little table by Mama's side of the bed, I can see the television, but not much else. I watch and watch quietly until I forget where I am and what time it is and hear myself laugh out loud at Johnny Carson. He has put on a silly hat and robe and is waving a magic wand. For a second everything in the room is quiet, and then Daddy swoops down from nowhere and asks me what I am doing, how did I get under this table, why am I not in bed. He is trying to be serious, but he and Mama are laughing even while they try to pretend to be mad. Daddy reaches for me and says, I AM GOING TO SPANK YOU! But I am already running, giggling so loud I can hear myself echo through our dark house, my socks sliding against the wood floor as I make my way to my bed.

When I am almost there, when my feet slide over the threshold of my bedroom door, Daddy catches me and swings me up over his shoulder, tickling me and telling me I should have been asleep long ago. I can barely breathe I am so excited. It is past my bedtime and I am out of breath and high in my daddy's arms, caught doing something I shouldn't. My heart races as I squirm to get down. Will Daddy really spank me? When we get to the edge of my bed, Daddy stands there for a few seconds, letting me writhe around in his strong arms. When I quiet down a bit, he smacks my upturned butt, his big hand coming down soft but firm on my tush. We both laugh and laugh at our hysterical game, and after he throws me down on my bed and tucks me in, kissing my forehead and telling me that I am the best daughter in the whole world and he loves me, I lie awake for a few minutes, a grin spread wide across my face.

It is poker night at our house. Daddy and a bunch of other men sit around the dark wood captain's table in the kitchen, laughing and smoking. Each player has a brightly colored package of cigarettes close by, a red or blue box that says Vantage, Winston, or Kool. Until it is time for me to take a bath, I sit on Daddy's lap picking up red, blue, and white plastic poker chips and dropping them into slots in the round caddy. It is hot and I'm wearing one of Daddy's tee shirts that comes to my knees. The back door is open. It is pitch black outside. Steamy pockets of air seep in through the screen.

Mama walks into the kitchen to put her big, brown tea mug in the sink. She wants to know why they aren't playing over at Doc Harmon's place, in the room behind his drugstore, like they usually do. The men, Daddy's law partners, one of whom will later become the first black judge in the state, and another the first black elected official, and a few other white civil rights workers from the North like Daddy, chuckle, glance at each other from behind their cards. "What's the matter, Alice, you don't like us over here? Hmmph. And we heard you wanted your husband at home for a change."

But Mama isn't fooled. She sees the rifle leaned up against the wall behind Daddy. The Klan must have left one of their calling cards: a white rectangle with two eyes shining through a pointed hood, THE KLAN IS WATCHING YOU in red letters underneath. She eyes the screen door, checks to see that it's locked, while my naked mosquito-bitten legs swing carelessly back and forth from up high on Daddy's lap.

Before I go to sleep, Daddy takes a "story break" from his poker game to tell me my favorite story about the man who lines up all the little girls in the world and asks my father to choose one. In my mind the guy who lines us all up looks like the guy on television, the man from *The Price Is Right*. Mr. Price Is Right beckons for my father to "step right up" and have a look at "all the girls in the world." My father walks up slowly, cautiously looking at Mr. Price Is Right as he puts his hand on my father's elbow. "Mr. Leventhal," he says, "you can have your pick of any girl you want. I have some of the best and brightest right here." For a second my father mocks interest. "Really?" But then Mr. Price Is Right shows his cards. "Yep. The only catch is that I want to keep Rebecca for myself."

Suddenly my father's body stiffens up and he shakes his head adamantly. "Oh no," says Daddy, "that won't do at all." And then he's angry. "Where is she?" he demands, already starting to walk down the line of little girls stretched out seemingly forever. "Where is my Rebecca?" Mr. Price Is Right doesn't know what to say. He hopes that if he doesn't answer, my father won't find me and he'll be able to keep me. But, my father says, turning to me all tucked into my jungle sheets, what Mr. Price Is Right doesn't know is that my father will always be able to find me, he's my father and I'm his daughter. We can always find each other.

So he walks and walks down the long line of little girls of every size and color, each girl calling out to him and trying to convince him to take them, until at last he finds me. His eyes light up as he takes my hand and leads me out of the line. Of course, Mr. Price Is Right runs over and tries once more to convince my father to leave me. "Oh please, Mr. Leventhal, look at all these other girls. Surely one of them will be just as good a daughter for you?" But my father is firm, shaking his head no and smiling a secret smile into my ecstatic face. "Come on, Rebecca," he says, "let's go home."

W hen they meet in 1965 in Jackson, Mississippi, my parents are idealists, they are social activists, they are "movement folk." They believe in ideas, leaders, and the power of organized people working for change. They believe in justice and equality and freedom. My father is a liberal Jew who believes these abstractions can be realized through the swift, clean application of the Law. My mother believes they can be cultivated through the telling of stories, through the magic ability of words to redefine and create subjectivity. She herself is newly "Black." She and my father comprise an "interracial couple."

By the time they fall in love, my parents do not believe in the über-sanctity of family. They do not believe that blood must necessarily be thicker than water, because water is what they are to each other, and they will be together despite the objection of blood. In 1967, when my parents break all the rules and marry against laws that say they can't, they say that an individual should not be bound to the wishes of their family, race, state, or country. They say that love is the tie that binds, and not blood. In a photograph from their wedding day, they stand, brown and pale pink, inseparable, my mother's tiny five-foot-one-inch frame nestled birdlike within my father's protective embrace. Fearless, naive, breathtaking, they profess their shiny, outlaw love for all the world to see.

I am not a bastard, the product of a rape, the child of some white devil. I am a Movement Child. My parents tell me I can do anything I put my mind to, that I can be anything I want. They buy me Erector sets and building blocks, Tinkertoys and books, more and more books. Berenstain Bears, Dr. Seuss, Hans Christian Andersen. We are middle class. My mother puts a colorful patterned scarf on her head and throws parties for me in our backyard, under the carport, and beside the creek. She invites all of my friends over and watches over us as we roast hot dogs. She makes Kool-Aid and laughs when one of us kids does something cute or funny.

I am not tragic.

L ate one night during my first year at Yale, a WASP-looking Jewish student strolls into my room through the fire-exit door. He is drunk, and twirling a Swiss Army knife between his nimble, tennis-champion fingers. "Are you really black and Jewish?" he asks, slurring his words, pitching forward in an old raggedy armchair my roommate has covered with an equally raggedy white sheet. "How can that be possible?"

Maybe it is his drunkenness, or perhaps he is actually trying to see me, but this boy squints at me then, peering at my nose, my eyes, my hair. I stare back at him for a few moments, eyes flashing with rage, and then take the red knife from his tanned and tapered fingers. As he clutches at the air above him, I hold it back and tell him in a voice I want him to be sure is black that I think he'd better go.

But after he leaves through the (still) unlocked exit door, I sit for quite a while in the dark.

Am I possible?

BROOKLYN

Dear Louisa,

Mama and Daddy bought us a big house that is a total mess! A woman had been living here for fifty years and then she died right before we moved in. There are leaves covering the floors and dust and dirt on everything. Mama keeps saying there is pretty wood underneath somewhere, but I don't know if I believe it. I went upstairs to the fourth floor by myself today and saw the ghost of the old woman rocking in her rocking chair and looking out the back window into what Mama keeps calling her rose garden, but what is now just overgrown weeds and bushes. I don't think I want to go up there anymore.

I have a new best friend, her name is Karen and she lives next door to us. Her father is a doctor and her mom lets us eat marshmallow Fluff. I broke my two front teeth at her birthday party. I had to pee really bad and I was pulling down my pants and running into the bathroom at the same time. I have a lot of new friends. There's Karen and her brother Glenn, a girl named Heather and her brother John, and a kid named Noah who rammed his Big Wheel into my bike when I was trying to learn without training wheels.

Mama says I am going to spend the summer with you and your parents on Long Island. She says she and Daddy have to strip the paint off the shutters in the house and the smell wouldn't be good for me. We have to buy a bathing suit for me because the one I had in Jackson doesn't fit anymore. Can I bring my cat Willis?

Love always,

Rebecca Grant Leventhal

Dear Mama,

You asked me what being at Grandma Miriam's house is like. Well, when Daddy drops me off, Grandma pulls me inside her door in a hurry, so that the air conditioning doesn't get out. Then we walk through that little room with red carpet and the piano in it and past all the pictures of Daddy at his bar mitzvah and blind Great-grandpa Samuel standing all stiff in a tuxedo, and Grandma on her wedding day and me in my sundress that I wore when we lived on Rockdale and Uncle Joel in the navy, through the living room and into the kitchen. If Great-grandma Jennie is there, I say hello to her even though she doesn't talk to me.

Usually Grandma wants me to eat right away, but she doesn't ever have a lot of food, so I either have boiled chicken (yuck!), or she heats up some frozen cheese blintzes. She opens out one of those TV trays for me and sets it up in front of the big TV in the living room. Then she makes sure the air conditioning is up high enough and goes into Daddy's old room to set up my bed on the pull-out sofa. I don't know why she makes it up since I always sleep with her, but I like having it to put all my stuff on. I probably shouldn't tell you this but then she lets me watch TV until we wash up to go to bed.

Today, me and Grandma and her best friend Ruth Glickstein sat outside on the green plastic folding chairs we usually take to the boardwalk. All of us worked on something. I am crocheting a little round thing that Grandma can stand her heavy dolls on so that they won't scratch the furniture. Ruth is knitting a sweater for her daughter, and I don't know what Grandma is making because she never sits still long enough to get very far. She is always jumping up and saying it's too hot to sit, and today she got into a fight with Aurora, her next-door neighbor. She said Aurora's son didn't put the garbage out right, and she started screaming at her from inside the gate. Aurora screamed right back, and when Grandma sat back down she said something about Aurora and her son not being clean. I think she also said something about them being Puerto Rican, but I didn't really get that part.

Yesterday Grandma took me shopping on Brighton Beach Avenue for a pocketbook. She says I'm old enough for one and I need one to carry all my personal things in. I guess like my crocheting and stuff. Then she took me to the movies.

I would write more, but Daddy is here to pick me up and he says I can tell you all this stuff when you get home from your trip.

I love you.

Trouper

D ear Louisa Patchogue Floyd,
      Daddy got mugged today while he was walking with his

briefcase from the D train stop right by our house. When he walked in the front door he looked hunched over and tired, like he needed to sit down. Mama wrapped her arms around his head and made him tell her what happened. Daddy tried to pretend like it was no big thing, but I could tell he was scared. He said two guys came up, one in front of him and one behind and they asked him for his wallet. One of the guys had a knife.

Mama said, What did you do? And Daddy said, I gave them my wallet, like what else was he going to do. Then he rubbed his face with his hands the way he does when he's tired.

They were quiet for a long time after that. Then Daddy picked his briefcase up off the floor and walked upstairs. I got Willis and took her to my room.

Write back!

Rebecca

Dear Mama,
  Today Grandma and I went to see Great-grandma Jennie at her house, on our way to Dr. Mixner's office across the street. Great-grandma Jennie is so old and her house smells bad. When I am there with Grandma I sit in the empty chair in the kitchen, the one that is a stepstool, too, while Grandma rushes around doing things. She checks her medicine, she makes sure she has had enough to eat, she asks about the woman who comes in to help. She is always telling her what she should be doing. "Mama," she says, yelling because I don't think Great-grandma can hear very well, "why did you put this chicken in the freezer?" "Mama, if you don't take this medicine you'll be very very sick."

Every time we come Grandma asks Great-grandma Jennie about Elsie or another one of her sisters. She asks if they have called or sent a check or anything. When Great-grandma says no Grandma shakes her head and laughs a little. "They never do anything, my rotten sisters, would you believe it? Not even a phone call. They just leave everything to me to do. My smart, rich sisters can't even call to see if their own mother is all right." And then she says something in Yiddish that I don't understand and throws her hands up in the air.

Great-grandma Jennie doesn't talk to me when I am in her house. It's like I am just a little girl in the chair by the kitchen door. Grandma always says, "Mama, see I brought Rebecca to see you. See Mama, Rebecca." Sometimes Great-grandma Jennie looks over at me but usually she doesn't, she doesn't even blink, she just keeps staring straight ahead with her ears pricked up and her nose in the air, like she's trying to hear Grandma as she moves around the house. Sometimes I wonder if she is blind.

When it is time to go Grandma comes back to me. She says, "Let's go Rebecca, we can't be late for the dentist." She shouts out really loud, "Goodbye Mama," and then she slams the door shut and double locks it behind her.

Did my granny have to take care of her mother like Grandma does?

Trouper

Dear Louisa Patchogue Floyd,
     The eggs in our incubator at school hatched! Well, most of them anyway. Some of the chicks died before they were born,

inside their eggs. Mrs. Spilken says that not all creatures make it past the egg stage, even if they have a real mother. That was kind of sad, but the chicks that lived are soft and they smell like seeds and straw.

Mama and Daddy had a big fight a few days ago. Mama wanted to go to the Botanic Gardens and Daddy wanted to sleep and she said he always sleeps or works and never does anything she wants to do and he didn't say anything. When he didn't say anything for a long time, she stopped talking and went downstairs. The next day Daddy and I went shopping for a present for her and he picked out a pot. I thought she would like it because it had pretty flowers painted on it and it was brown and blue, colors Mama likes. When we got home Mama had painted the kitchen cabinets bright red and when Daddy gave her the pot she looked at him kind of funny and said, "You got me a cooking pot for my birthday?" and just put it down on the table without taking it out of the box.

After they both went upstairs, I went inside one of the cabinets Mama had just painted and found out I could fit, so I got Willis and closed the door and sat there for a while.

Write back!
Love,
Rebecca Grant Walker Leventhal

Great-grandma Jennie came from Russia, from a little town called Kiev, but she won't admit this to me even though I am her great-granddaughter and writing a report on my oldest living family member for school. At Grandma's house she won't look at me when I ask her this question, but I know she hears me because her face looks tight, like someone is pulling her ears back behind her head. And even though she is sitting still in her chair, the one with the little gold-flecked Formica trays on either side instead of arm-rests, her swollen arthritic fingers clutch at the steel tubing of her walker.

I put down the pencil I was holding and study Great-grandma's feet, the chafed, pinkish-white skin at her ankles, the way the little folds droop onto the edges of her black orthopedic shoes. I want to ask another question, but instead I get up from the table and go stand as close as I can to Grandma, pulling at her apron while she moves around the kitchen.

As Grandma pulls out one of the tin TV trays with the chipping enamel roses on top from alongside the oven and snaps it into place in front of her mother's chair, she tells me that Great-grandma Jennie was a little girl when she came to this country and doesn't remember the answers to the questions I ask. I nod my head but still don't understand why Great-grandma Jennie is always so angry, why she hardly ever looks at or talks to me. I feel invisible, present but also not, like I am floating.

When my father comes to pick me up later, he tells me that I am too young to understand Great-grandma Jennie's fear of being from Russia, her fear that she'll be labeled a Communist and put in jail, or deported. He tells me I am too young to understand about the pogroms Great-grandma Jennie ran from, the burning of Jewish villages, homes, people. He says that this desire to protect me, and not anything else, is behind her angry silence.

I am not too young to feel shut out.

I wonder what it is like to harbor a primal loyalty to your family: grandmothers, aunts, uncles, brothers. To put them, those others connected to you by birth, by name, before those you choose to claim as your own. To consider the ones you were born with your first layer of protection, your inner sanctum, the blood in which you live that cannot be diluted by the water you drink. I am fascinated by this emotion, this human device that creates purpose and meaning, self and other. Is it something we are born with, or is this subtle belonging cultivated, a by-product of the endless repetition of rituals: setting the table, driving to school, walking the dog?

For many years I tell people whom I think will be shocked about my Slavic, Jewish ancestry. I get a strange, sadistic pleasure from watching their faces contort as they reconsider the woman who was more easily dismissible as Puerto Rican or Arab. On the subway, surrounded by Hasidim crouched xenophobically over their Bibles, I have to sit on my hands and bite my tongue to keep from shouting out, "I know your story!" I don't feel loyalty as much as an irrational, childlike desire to burst their suffocating illusions of purity.

I want to be recognized as family.

BROOKLYN

We leave Jackson in the summertime, I remember, because on moving day I wear my favorite red sundress, the one my mother loves, with the yellow spaghetti straps that tie at my shoulders. Mama and Daddy stay up late the night before making piles of clothes to give away, writing "study" and "kitchen" and "bedroom" on big brown cartons. We wake up while it is still cool, to "get an early start," and spend the dawn loading up our old battered red Volvo.

After the sewing machine and Mama's typewriter, Daddy carries out the last suitcase, a boxy brown suede thing his law partners gave him as a going-away present, his name and the address of the law firm etched onto its aluminum lock. Mama has a lamp in one hand and a framed picture, Modigliani's "Alice," in the other. I lug my own little suitcase, a hard red one Mama bought me for trips, which I already know how to pack. It swings clumsily from side to side at my hip as I struggle to heave it along, my brown strappy sandals slapping the walkway to the car, my straw hat from Cuba shielding my eager face from the sun.

In Brooklyn my life is no longer simple, Southern, and peopled with the same half-dozen earnest faces. Grown-ups aren't "in the movement" but have regular jobs they go to on the subway every day. When I go out to play I have to watch out for the constant stream of cars that go whizzing by our house, and there are what seems like a million more people in our greatly expanded universe. Vinnie the butcher, the Chinese couple who manage the Szechuan restaurant where we have barbequed spare ribs every weekend, the Carrs who live across the street.

Instead of walking down the street to Mrs. Cornelius's house, I spend afternoons and evenings after school either at Mrs. Hunt and Debbie Perez's dark brownstone across the street or tooling around the tiny three-bedroom bungalow in Brighton Beach that my father grew up in. Moving from household to household is like switching between radio stations: Each type of music calls for a different dance, but it all exists simultaneously, on the same dial. Doing the switching is easy, it's figuring out how one relates to the other that is hard.

Mrs. Hunt is old and short and has bluish eyes that are always running. She smells like vanilla and crumbling mothballs, wears a wig that doesn't fit and the same outfit every day: thick orange polyester pants with a matching vest over a purple and green paisley polyester shirt.

Mrs. Hunt speaks to me in Spanish, and the universal language, food. *Mi'ja* she calls me when I walk into her house, hugging me to her breast and then leading me to the kitchen, *ven a comer*. Her granddaughter Debbie teaches me how to slow dance by the light of dark red and green glass candles with the Virgin of Guadalupe painted on their slick sides. When Mrs. Hunt is in bed with her arthritis, Debbie puts "Love to Love You Baby" or "My Cherie Amour" on the record player and has me practice French-kissing my reflection on the mirrored panels above the eight-track, right below a velvet painting of Jesus weeping under his crown of thorns.

My grandma is totally different, but so much the same. Leading me into the kitchen, she calls me *bubbeleh, tchotchkeleh,* and her favorite, oldest grandchild. On weekends she takes me to the Oceana movie theater. We see *Fantasia* and a movie about the real Noah's ark, which she says is important for me to see because I am Jewish. "Don't ever forget," she says afterward as we walk under the el on Brighton Beach Avenue on our way home, "you're a Jew! I don't care what Mama and Daddy say."

Not that she is so religious. As far as I can tell, aside from herself and an old menorah, the only thing Jewish about her is the broken Yiddish she sometimes speaks to Great-grandma Jennie. That and the illustrated Old Testament books she gives me to read; the books that show a bearded white Moses leading the Jews out of Egypt, that she ordered for $3.95 from a tear-out ad in *TV Guide.*

And there is still another woman who mothers me after school in Brooklyn, a woman who takes me home to her parents' house on Long Island when summer comes and the city is unbearable with heat and dirt and overpowering humidity. Louisa is a beautiful, sturdy, green-eyed law student. She is always smiling, and when I am with her I feel like I am on the verge of all that is sexy and exciting and powerful about being a girl.

A few times a week Louisa and I throw pails and shovels and

blow-up rafts and flip-flops and towels into the backseat of her hatchback and speed off barefoot to the beach. Once we hit the highway, she turns the music up really loud, both of us looking straight ahead through the windshield, and we sing along to Bob Dylan and Aretha Franklin, bobbing our heads. One day on our way out of the city, she buys me my first sunglasses, a bright yellow plastic pair from the children's rack at Kmart, and my first bikini, four navy blue triangles laced together with a white ribbon.

From Louisa I learn how to put my shades on and be cool, to smile at the boys who sidle up alongside our car on the highway but pay them no mind. From Louisa I learn to move like I am important, in control; as if I, Rebecca, belong.

Years later, in junior high, when black girls named Susan and Donna and Monique threaten to beat me up for "acting like a white girl," it is this attitude they must be talking about. I act like I am entitled to bliss, like I am not afraid of what the world has to offer. When light-skinned Jeffrey French and the cute Peruvian boy with the black wavy hair and the smile that lights up the hallway try to talk to me, and when I answer all the questions correctly in Mrs. Thompson's math class, it does not occur to me that I am taking something away from the other, darker-skinned girls, that I am doing something to them that feels like betrayal. What I do know is that at three o'clock, when I run terrified out the cafeteria doors to the safety of the school bus taking me home, my best friend Lena, a white girl who lives across the street and rides the bus back and forth to school with me every day, is nowhere to be found.

this is the last time I will see my father
naked this is the last time I will see my
father naked this is the last time I will
see my father naked this is the last time
I will see my father naked this is the
last time I will see my father naked this
is the last time I will see my father
naked this is the last time I will see my
father naked this is the last time I will
see my father naked this is the last time
I will see my father naked this is the
last time I will see my father naked this
is the last time I will see my father
naked this is the last time I will see my
father naked this is the last time I will
see my father naked this is the last time
I will see my father naked this is the
last time I will see my father naked this
is the last time I will see my father

M y father's brother Jackie and my mother's brother Bobby are my two favorite uncles. Uncle Jackie is my favorite because he always asks about my mother. Even more than that, I like his sweet musky man smell, his habit of playing with my hair when we are seated at the Passover seder table together, the way he absentmindedly twirls my fat curls around and around his short, thick fingers. He is not afraid to touch me, to be close to me.

There is also the fact that he, a nice Jewish boy from Brooklyn, is married to my aunt Lisa, a nice Italian Catholic girl from Staten Island, so there is a kind of harmonious discord in their house, a bicultural theme that feels familiar. There are huge Christmases at Uncle Jackie's house, with lit-up plastic mangers and Santas and elves scattered on the front lawn. There are communion parties for his three children filled with Italian friends and relatives named Angie and Marco. Aunt Lisa's mother is dead, but her father is sometimes there, muttering in Italian and chain-smoking in front of football on the television.

There are also good presents for birthdays and Chanukah at

Uncle Jackie's house, boxes and boxes of toy trains and dolls and baseball mitts and clothes. There are presents at my house, too, but they are about developing my mind, or my coordination, or my identity as a non-gender-defined child. Mama buys me books, a Hula-Hoop, an Etch A Sketch, or a journal. Daddy buys me board games, puzzles, magic tricks, and workbooks that help me improve my math. At Uncle Jackie's I get the Jordache and Sergio Valente jeans that Mama refused to buy me because they are too expensive and which Aunt Lisa's best friend Eileen has in bulk, and another year Aunt Lisa gives me my favorite outfit ever, a dark blue corduroy skirt and matching vest from Abraham & Straus that I wear on special occasions for two years straight.

I don't remember my mother ever being at Aunt Lisa and Uncle Jackie's house. I can't picture her there at the big white dining room table, passing the ravioli or the little Italian pastries at the end of the meal, listening to my grandmother kvetch about how ungrateful her daughters-in-law are and how tragic it is that she isn't ever going to have Jewish grandchildren because her sons married shiksas. I imagine that if my mother were there she would be unbearably sensitive, masked, edgy. It would be too stressful for her to sit and pretend that she felt comfortable and embraced, welcomed like any other family member. As if race, and hers in particular, was not an issue.

That it is an issue is undeniable, her absence confirms it, and I am far from oblivious. Nights at Uncle Jackie's I miss my mother's deep, melodious laughter floating alongside my father's, her elegant brown hands pooh-poohing my grandmother's ridiculous assertions, her warm voice complimenting my aunt Lisa on her antipasto. Her presence at the table would grant me the great luxury of being able to love my family members unreservedly, to take them irrevocably as my own. As it is, the specter of my mother, of race, really, and the inability of my relatives to deal with it, leaves me somewhere on the periphery of my own experience, unable to commit to fully being there. Haunted by her absence, I pull back cautiously and feel, even as I laugh and play with my cousins, as if some part of me is alien to the others, as if I am in the family through some kind of affirmative-action plan and don't entirely belong.

Instead of screaming this out at the grown-ups while they play Tonk and Gin with the blue cards Grandma has brought home from one of her many bookkeeping jobs, I lock myself in the little downstairs bathroom. After pushing in the brass button in the door handle, I let my mind take over, studying every item in the room: the burgundy and navy blue hand towels, which I can tell are new because they have that slick, never-been-washed feeling; the bar of Camay soap I know my mother won't like because the fragrance is too strong and artificial-smelling; the balled-up pieces of tissue in the plastic wastebasket that must be Grandma's because she has some kind of sinus infection; the Band-Aids and antiseptic ointments and half-filled prescription bottles, a few of which are expired, in the medicine chest. By the time I splash my face with cold water and attach some kind of meaning to everything around me, someone else is at the door, wanting to come in. Either that or my aunt Lisa is knocking, calling to me with her Jewish-inflected Italian accent, "Hey, Rebecca! Whaddaya doing in there?"

I don't remember Uncle Jackie and Aunt Lisa ever coming to our house, either. Where would they have sat, on one of the two red love seats in the parlor, or on the big beige corduroy sofa in the living room? How would they have moved among the dark wood and endless cases of books; how would my giddy, frenetic cousins have interpreted the quiet stillness my mother kept in our house, the emphasis on beauty and color and handmade things? Could they tune into our domestic frequency with the ease with which I was expected to tune into theirs?

When I run into one of my cousins years later in the gritty dark green of the Fourteenth Street subway station, we stand awkwardly, trying to bridge some gulf neither of us knows how to acknowledge but which neither of us can deny. He, all grown up with horn-rimmed glasses and in his first year of law school, tells me about the house he's renting on Fire Island. I fumble for my token and get out something about an article I am writing and a trip I've just taken, but I notice that I hold back, still unable to commit to fully being there. On the train I ponder the distance between us, the way I feel closeted around him, not my real self. I think about the fact that I can see him clearly, from childhood to now, going and coming back to that house on Bridgewater Lane I know so well. I can see both his mother and his father in his eyes and his cheekbones and his walk, and I know their dreams for him firsthand.

His is a story that is coherent to me, linear, accessible, plain. But mine is half alien to him, blurry, imagined, incomplete. He knows my father well but has only heard stories about my mother. To bridge the distance I must choose to share with him the part he doesn't know, and I'm not sure that I trust him. Because keeping a part of myself held back is what I've done to cope for the last twenty years, opting instead to be partially known, reservedly intimate, I have no idea if I can tolerate what might be a less than accepting response. Protecting myself, I decide I'd rather not know if my cousin is just another racist hick from Staten Island. When we see each other at family dinners, we hug, make small talk, and avoid looking too deeply into each other's eyes.

D addy is in the bathtub and I am standing at the sink. The bathtub has clawed feet, the sink is on an ancient Victorian pedestal, and the walls are covered with peeling green paint Mama and Daddy have yet to strip. A single bare bulb with a chain hangs from the ceiling. I am standing naked on tiptoe and the water is running cold onto my fingers. Daddy is lying in hot water, I can see the steam rising up from the tub and from his pale pink, hairy body. His feet rest on the lip above the faucet, his head is back.

Today I am not taking a bath with him, though I do sometimes. I am just in the bathroom with him. I wash as he washes, taking a sink-bath like my mother does sometimes, standing at the sink with her wash cloth, rubbing all the places I think are dirty with a soapy towel. We are both quiet, the only sound the running water and the drip drip of the faucet into the tub.

This is the last time I will see my father naked. This is the last time he and I will share the bathroom, the last time we both will be quiet and exposed in the same room together, when we will not have to speak to be connected. When just being in his presence is all I need.

who am I if I am not a Movement
Child? who am I if I am not a Move
ment Child? who am I if I am not
Movement Child? who am I if I am
not a Movement Child? who am I if
am not a Movement Child? who am
if I am not a Movement Child? who
am I if I am not a Movement Child
who am I if I am not a Movement
Child? who am I if I am not a Move
ment Child? who am I if I am not
Movement Child? who am I if I am
not a Movement Child? who am I if
am not a Movement Child? who am
I am not a Movement Child? who
am I if I am not a Movement Child
who am I if I am not a Movement
Child? who am I if I am not a Move
ent Child? who am I if I am not

MORPHOLOGY

My mother buys thick blood-red velvet curtains for my room. She says that very strong light comes through my windows and I need something very dark to keep the light out so I can sleep. At night I have nightmares. I see shadows behind the dark red curtains, lightning bolts, thunder. My anxiety about not being able to see what is behind the curtains keeps me stock still and rigid in my bed, arms pinned at my sides, sweating. The only thing that makes bed bearable is my fantasy that Abraham Lincoln, who I know so well from his picture on my NAACP Lifetime Membership plaque, will come and save me if something reaches in to snatch me from the other side of the curtains.

After a few months my mother moves the king-size bed into my room, and then she sleeps with me in it, crying every night before she falls asleep. I do not understand why she is crying. I do not understand why my daddy now goes out late at night, why he comes into my room to kiss my mother and me goodnight. How he can kiss her without feeling the wetness on her cheeks, how he can leave me here in this room, in this bed with my mother who has only my little arms wrapped around her neck to comfort her.

Night after night Mama and I are tucked into our king-size bed on the warm side of the blood-red velvet curtains, and night after night I fall asleep with my pudgy copper arms wrapped around her neck. As we drift out of consciousness, I feel the ether of my spirit meet the ether of hers and become all tangled up. As I fall asleep I do not know where she starts and I begin. I do know that my mama is hurting and that what I have to give to stop that hurting is myself: my arms, my warmth, my little hands on the side of her face. I no longer am only for myself, but now I'm for her, too. I must be strong. I learn how to forget myself, to take my cues from her, to watch carefully so that I can know what to do.

A woman with straight black hair, wearing a cowl-neck sweater and knee-high suede boots, rings the bell at our house one night as Daddy reads me a story in front of the fireplace. When he answers the door, he acts surprised. Mama is out giving a lecture, away overnight, and Daddy is being Daddy and Mama, he is reading to me and afterward will take me upstairs and tuck me into bed. But this woman comes in and she has brought marshmallows, and so Daddy instead of putting me to sleep lets me stay up later than he would if Mama were home and I roast marshmallows in front of the fireplace as Daddy and this woman talk quietly on the little red loveseat.

This is the woman Daddy will marry in a year's time. The big Jewish wedding with the big, blue velvet huppah and wall-to-wall Jewish people will take place on this very floor of our house, in front of this fireplace. The reception room, where my stepmother will pour Perriet-Jouët champagne for her guests and where I will run to sneak and hide in the back staircase by the old dumbwaiter that doesn't work, is none other than my mother's study. But now her big desk is gone, all her books and papers are gone, and my new stepmother's old oak breakfront is against the wall and guests are sitting on the red loveseat that my parents sat me down on to tell me they were getting a divorce.

My father still treats me like a child even though he expects me to understand all kinds of things I have no way of understanding. Like sleeping over at his new girlfriend's house on her sofa. Like letting this new woman pick me up from school and take me shopping. This I do not understand, but for my daddy, I pretend to understand. I say, Everything is okay. I like this sofa, I like this woman, I like this house, I like the food she cooks. I say, Daddy, keep choosing me because I am perfect because I don't make you feel guilty, I don't express my fear, my rage, my hurt. I say only, Yes, Daddy, I like her, let's go fly kites in Central Park. Yes, Daddy, it is okay that you are breaking my heart with this woman I don't know, letting her into my life, letting her buy me presents, letting me love her.

In my bed behind the blood-red curtains I learn not to be a child. I watch as my mother's soft, curvy brown body is replaced by my stepmother's thin, pointy white one. This new mother tells me to stay in my own room, that I am too old to climb into what was my parents' bed in the middle of the night. But after so many nights of lying behind those curtains with my mother, to lie there alone is terrifying. There is no one in my big bed to keep me warm, and so I begin to touch myself for warmth, for protection against whatever it is my mother wants to protect me from with those heavy blood-red curtains.

Late at night in my big bed I bunch the covers up, wrap them around my feet, and put pillows over my head to feel held in, to feel my mother again. I keep myself company with smooth, lonely touching, holding myself when no one else is available, warming the cold air that remains.

I don't remember my parents talking to each other much, or laughing or easily throwing their arms around each other's shoulders the way they must have when they were in love. By the time I am old enough to remember them together, it is mostly the silences that I remember, the almost eerie calm. They tell me later that they fought behind closed doors, late at night after I had gone to bed. They fought about my father's relentless obsession with his work, his single-minded focus on his clients and the law that took him away from home and from my mother and the things she liked to do. They wrestled over my mother's longings, her real need for beauty and freedom and poetic companionship.

Like any normal couple, I suppose, my parents change, perhaps discovering the ways in which they are longer compatible, but also the real world begins to bleed into the margins of their idealistic love. Even though Daddy goes off to work at the NAACP Legal Defense Fund every day and Mama keeps writing her books about black people and their experiences, they are no longer held together by a web of folk committed to the transgressive nature of their union.

With the rise of Black Power, my parents' interracial defiance, so in tune with the radicalism of Dr. King and civil rights, is suddenly suspect. Black-on-black love is the new recipe for revolution, mulatto half-breeds are tainted with the blood of the oppressor, and being down means proving how black you are, how willing to fight, how easily you can turn your back on those who have kept black folks enslaved for so long. My father, once an ally, is, overnight, recast as an interloper. My mother, having once found refuge in a love that is unfashionable, may no longer have been willing to make the sacrifice.

And then Feminism, with a capital F, codified Feminism, "movement" Feminism, as opposed to the feminism that has always lived under our roof and that teaches me I can be whatever I want, dresses me in green and red corduroy jumpers instead of pink dresses, gives me books on Sojourner Truth and by Louisa May Alcott and tells me I can go to Harvard, comes to our house. Mama joins a group of black women writers who call themselves the Sisterhood and takes a position at *Ms.* magazine. It isn't that my mother wasn't feminist before, but now she is surrounded by the Feminism she is helping to create. This historical moment is about options, about formulating a life defined not by male desire but by female courage. Which is exactly what it takes to leave my father.

The only problem, of course, is me. My little copper-colored body that held so much promise and broke so many rules. I no longer make sense. I am a remnant, a throwaway, a painful reminder of a happier and more optimistic but ultimately unsustainable time.

Who am I if I am not a Movement Child?

E ach morning before school I look for my mother's purse. Velvety blue corduroy or stiff brown leather, the one she carried before going to sleep is usually hanging from one of the chairs in the living room, or else it is by her desk in the bedroom, and I will have to be super quiet or risk waking her up. Once I find it I stick my hand inside, pushing my fingers all the way down to the bottom and holding all the contents to one side while the change collects in a cool mound on the other. I scoop up quarters, nickels, and dimes I hope my mother has forgotten about, filling my pockets until they are bulging and heavy.

After school one day I go to my friend Sarah's house. Her father is black and her mother is white and they live in a big brownstone that reminds me on the outside of the one I still live in on weekends, with my dad and stepmother. Inside, Sarah has a loft bed and a brother and a sister and the walls of their kitchen and living room are painted a warm, cheerful orange. There are books and newspapers scattered on the floor in the living room next to Sarah's dolls and xylophone, and the phone keeps ringing and when Sarah's mom answers it she yells up the stairs to Sarah's older sister to pick it up.

When I go into Sarah's house something inside of me freezes up and I walk around numb, trying to pretend that I'm okay when I'm really not. When we go up to her room and I stand by the door, looking at everything she has with what I hope doesn't look like envy but is, Sarah looks at me funny and then climbs up into her big safe loft bed, out of my sight. I don't stay long. I can't figure out what to do there, how to be, because my feelings of longing are so strong. I want to be Sarah. I want to live in this big, warm, normal house where there is noise all around and mess and a big high bed for me in the center of it all. I think, something must be wrong with me that I can't have this, that I can't have what Sarah has.

When I leave her house I walk straight to the candy and newspaper store on the corner and buy six packs of bubble gum in all different flavors with the money from my mother's purse. Before I reach the door to our apartment, before pulling out my key and letting myself in, I have chewed the sugar out of a whole pack of strawberry Bubblicious. My jaw aches and I can feel the sugar boring into my teeth but I can't stop putting the rubbery cubes into my mouth, draining the sugar out of them and then spitting the wad out into the little straw wastepaper basket by my bed. By the time my mother gets home, I have finished all six packs.

I stop making sense in third grade. Right after my parents sit me down and tell me they are not getting along, that me and Mama are going to move to another neighborhood and Daddy will come to pick me up on weekends. They might as well have told me we were moving to live with penguins on the North Pole, but I nod my head and help Mama pack books and generally move as if nothing is wrong, as if there isn't this big crack in the middle of the painting that is supposed to be my life.

Because we have to live on the tiny amount of money my mother makes writing, Mama and I move into a floor-through on the other side of Prospect Park one fourth the size of our house on Midwood. My room is the size of the bathroom in the old house, with just a bed and a tall, skinny chest of drawers which I climb on a lot, sometimes sitting on top and staring out the window for hours at the trees blowing and the people walking by. When Mama comes home from work, she cooks dinner for us, scrambled eggs and bacon, or a magic soup she learned how to make from her father out of whatever vegetables we have in the fridge tossed into chicken broth.

While she cooks I do homework, or I stretch out on the blue velvet couch in our living room, listening to music Mama asks me to put on the phonograph to drown out the sounds that come muffled through our ceiling: another half-black half-white child screaming, wrestling with his white mother who always looks exhausted when I see her in the hallway. Mama and I listen to Phoebe Snow singing "Teach Me Tonight," or the Beatles singing "Come Together," or our favorite, the soundtrack from *Jesus Christ Superstar.*

Late at night we talk quietly in the bathroom, me handing her the Vitabath and washing her back, the bright orange washcloth huge in my eight-year-old hand. In the mornings I climb into her bed and press my face against the soft blue flannel of her nightgown, inhaling her clean, spicy scent. One cold night we sit upright in the bed with the tall wooden headboard, and she dictates to me how she wants her funeral. You have to make sure it is this way, she says, and I nod. There should be a party, she says, smoothing lotion down one arm. Lots of people dancing. She pauses as I write that down on the legal pad. And don't let them put me in a big ugly coffin. N-o u-g-l-y c-of-f-i-n, I write. I should be buried in a simple pine box and S-t-e-v-i-e W-o-n-d-e-r should be playing over the PA.

I don't know. Mama put me in this new school over here near where we live now, she and me in three rooms the size of one of the floors of our old house, mine and Mama and Daddy's house. We went to the little office on the first floor with Mama's new boyfriend and she filled out the papers and the people looked me up and down and shuffled some other papers, and then Mama said I needed to be in the gifted class and the woman behind the desk looked at me again, harder, like she was trying to see through to my brain. And then I was in a classroom with Mrs. Leone helping her staple orange leaves made out of construction paper to the wall around the blackboard. And then I was walking down the hallway with my new class, following the green line painted on the waxy concrete floor, and then we were in the auditorium for assembly and then I was in Mr. Ward's music class, just like that.

It is dark in Mr. Ward's music room. There is wood on the walls, which is weird because our school, PS 321, is made of cement and other hard materials, like metal, which is in skinny bars on the windows. Mama's new boyfriend says this is because our

school was built in the fifties, when they thought you could prepare for an A-bomb. Mr. Ward is handing out instruments from a
big cardboard box next to his piano bench. He tries to distribute
them evenly throughout the room, so it's not just the kids in front
who get the good instruments, but there are way more of us than
there are cymbals and drums and guitars so most of us get plastic
yellow recorders with one part missing.

I feel out of my element here in Mr. Ward's class, like everyone
knows how to make music but me, even though I can tell by the
way the other kids are banging and blowing that this is not true.
It is true that I am much more comfortable in reading class, where
I whiz through the SRA colors like a bat out of hell. I'm in the
third grade, but according to the purple and red folders I am up
to in SRA, I read at the seventh-grade level. I get one hundreds on
all of my spelling tests, and Mrs. Leone puts them up on the closet
doors next to the SRA folders at the back of the room.

Sometimes when I am in her class I feel like it's just me and
her in the room and none of the other kids is there at all. It's sort
of like that in Mr. Ward's class, too, except I don't feel like I'm here
with Mr. Ward. Here I'm just alone with all of these other kids
with names and faces but not much else. When Mr. Ward tells me
to, I put my fingertips on a couple of the holes and blow through
the mouthpiece of my recorder. I try to focus on what Mr. Ward
is saying, but he's not teaching us notes or chords or anything else
about music. He seems bored and aggravated, especially by the
boys in the back who won't be quiet and do what he says. When
everyone starts playing their instruments and making an awful,
loud, horrible noise that hurts my ears, Mr. Ward just spaces out

and looks at us like he doesn't know how we all got to be here together in the basement of some public school in Brooklyn.

Bryan Katon is sitting with his legs crossed on my left, closer to the music stands by the door, beating on a drum. If I close my eyes I can almost smell him. Bryan has milky white skin and red freckles. He has sandy brown hair that always falls in front of his eyes, like Linus on *Charlie Brown*. Bryan lives way out in Bay Ridge somewhere but his parents own the dry-cleaning store across the street from school, the one next to the pizza parlor where we all go for lunch. If I walk to school early enough I sometimes see Bryan getting out of a black car with his parents. He crosses the street and goes into school while his father rolls up the gate in front of the cleaners.

Bryan Katon is the boy I like. I don't know why I like him, I just do. I like the way he is kind of tough and has a lot of friends and talks in a choppy, offhand way, like he doesn't care if anyone is listening. I like the way his parents give him money when he asks for it. I like it that his mother and father are right across the street. The one time I go into Katon Cleaners with Bryan at lunchtime, it is all warm inside and his mother smiles when we come in and asks him why he is late, like she was worried. For a split second I imagine myself back behind the counter with her, getting lost in all the hanging skirts and blouses and suits, breathing in all those fumes and pressing my cheeks against the silky plastic bags. I imagine that she tells me to stop, that I could hurt myself, in that same worried voice.

.   .   .

I tell Sarah that Bryan Katon is the boy I like. Sarah is my friend but I don't trust her all the way. This year I'm paranoid. I don't trust any of my friends all the way. Not Donna, not Siobhan, and not Jamie, who I sometimes meet on the corner in the mornings so we can walk to school together. I trust Karen but she lives by my old house and now she goes to a private school six blocks away and I never see her. I'm never sure what the new friends are going to do, if they are going to stop being my friends one day for no good reason, or what.

To protect myself, I start to buy my friends things with money I take from my mother's purse. I like the way it feels to pay for something at the register, to be able to give my friends something they want. I feel safer, older, bigger, knowing that they look to me as some kind of provider, even if it is only because I have the money: nickels and dimes and quarters paid out in bubble gum and sets of jacks and plastic-topped containers filled with goopy, green Slime.

And because I know things they don't, things I learn from reading books like *Forever,* by Judy Blume, which I bought for myself at the bookstore for $2.95. I know, for instance, that a penis can have a name and feel really soft and good inside of a girl. But this is something I am not supposed to know, only I don't know that I'm not supposed to know it until one day I am reading paragraphs from *Forever* to my friend Sasha. We are sitting in the front window of her mother's clothing store on Seventh Avenue, a couple of blocks up from the cleaners and the pizza parlor. There is sun coming in through the windows, and the floor underneath us is covered in this cushy beige carpet that makes me want to lie down and take a nap. I see Sasha's mother's feet walk over to where we are sitting and then I hear her ask to see what we are reading.

When I look up at Sasha's mother I see her looking at the book like the woman in the office at school looked at me, trying to see through to my brain. Then she tells me that Sasha isn't allowed to read books like *Forever* and I should go home because Sasha isn't allowed to play with me anymore. That's how I find out that I'm not supposed to know about boys putting their penises inside of girls' vaginas.

So Sarah tells Bryan and then Bryan tells me, in front of his friends, after school one day when it is cold and there is dirty gray snow on the ground and we all are leaving to go home, that he doesn't like black girls. Bryan Katon tells me that he doesn't like black girls. Bryan Katon, the boy that I like, tells me that he doesn't like black girls, and I think, with this big whoosh that turns my stomach upside down and almost knocks me over, is that what I am, a black girl? And that's when all the trouble starts, because suddenly I don't know what I am and I don't know how to be not what he thinks I am. I don't know how to be a not black girl.

My stepmother is a not black girl. When she picks me up on Fridays after school in her tall, brown suede boots for the weekend, I wait inside school a little longer, until I am sure Bryan is outside and will see me go over to her and be hugged by her. I want him to see her take my backpack from me and take my hand, and I want him to see me get into her car. And when my grandma Miriam comes to pick me up on other days I do the same thing, I make a big fuss in front of school so that he will see that I am related to not black girls.

I start to brush my hair straight, a hundred times every night before I go to sleep, like I see Jan Brady do on *The Brady Bunch.* Jan Brady is a not black girl. I roll my hair in pink rollers when I am at my grandma's house so that I will have bangs, so that my hair will look more like the not black girls in my class. And I tell my stepmother that I want the doll she says I should want, because all girls want dolls, and even though I have not ever had a baby doll and I am not all that interested in a plastic baby that eats colored mush and then poops it out, I think, this must be part of being a not black girl.

At school Mrs. Leone tells us that we, our class, are going to put on a play for the whole school. She tells us this from the front of the classroom, where she walks back and forth looking out at our faces. Some of you will make the sets for the show, some will make costumes, and some of you, she says, will act. The play is *The Wizard of Oz,* she says, and hands short rectangular stacks to the first person in each row to pass backward until we all have our own wad of mimeographed sheets to hold.

I rush through my pages, inhaling the sweet, tart, mediciny odor of the purplish blue ink. Who do I want to be? We read the whole play out loud, and everyone who wants to act tries different parts on, to see which one fits. Mrs. Leone has me try the Lion, Auntie Em, the Wizard himself. I do not notice that she has only not black girls read the words underneath Dorothy's name, I am too excited by the idea of acting, reading out loud, and making my voice change to match what I think each character should sound like. By the end of classtime it all is decided. I will play the Wicked Witch of the West.

I don't tell my mother too much about the play, and she doesn't ask. It isn't a big deal, I say, hoping she won't see through my mask of nonchalance; I don't want to hurt her. I don't want to lie, either, but how else am I going to convince her not to come to see me on Play Night? How else can I explain that Bryan Katon doesn't like black girls and if she comes he will definitely know that I am, in fact, a black girl, and all of my other efforts to be a not black girl will be washed away? How else can I stay with her and still leave?

On the night of the play, as I am trying on my black witch's cape and pointy hat for the umpteenth time, I beg her not to come. I will be too nervous, I say, I won't be able to remember my lines if you are there, I say. Please, Mama, don't come. She looks at me strangely, like the woman in the office did, trying to see through to my brain. I hold my breath but she doesn't push. She takes me at my word and I go, free, alone, out into the night. When I look out from the stage I can make out my grandmother's white face in the dark crowd. I think, Mama is not here, Mama is at home. I think, surely Bryan will see my grandmother. I think, surely Bryan will like me now.

At the end, when all the parents and teachers stand up and clap for us, I feel an unexpected sadness come into my body, a heat inching up from someplace underneath the skin on my face.

I picture Mama lying in her big bed by the window, alone, the lamp giving off a pool of yellow light as she reads, silently wondering about Play Night. Even though everyone says I was good, my mama, the one with the most important voice, can never say this to me.

Shame sticks to me like sweat.

I start to remember in shards, pieces of glass that rip my skin and leave marks. I find tight little cuts all over: one on my left breast, grazing the nipple, and one that starts just below my left eyebrow and runs across my nose to the light brown line of my upper lip. Another is on my back, burning from the base of my spine over the soft roundness of the right cheek of my behind. Yet another one, trying to scab, unable to heal, is buried on my scalp. These are memories like a broken bottle, memories I can't speak because the glass gets caught in my throat, ripping it, too. I circle these glinty flashes from above for days, weeks, before I can find a way to sit down with them alone in my room, in front of the computer. From my lofty perch they appear minor, mere scratches; it is only when I look closely that I see them for what they are: self-mutilations and battle scars.

In this process of remembering, I am surprised to find a clear trail of words lodged somewhere in the back of my brain, embedded in the tissue surrounding my heart, waiting to surface. I am not surprised to find that this surfacing gives me something I have always wanted, a story to go with this body. Before now, when I run into myself on top of my grandmother's piano or in the family album, I see only what others have told me was there. I see all the shiny adjectives: sunny, bright, warm, happy. Listening to friends of my parents, I nod, smile, and imagine a sweet child, naturally curious, naturally loving, yet what she has to do with me I haven't the faintest idea.

As they speak I let my mind go blank; it is so much easier to be an empty screen for their projections, so much easier to believe all those nice words than to try to reach back there and piece it all together. After all these years it is second nature to me, this negation of my own mind, my own heart, my own story. Pushing the corners of memory far back into the recesses, I say to myself again and again: They remember it better.

It is jarring to think that most of my life I have been defined by others, primarily reactive, going along with the prevailing view. It makes me feel younger now, new, and slightly terrified. Having to remember my own life means that I have to feel it, too. I have to pay attention to the thoughts that float, uninvited, to mind. I have to heed the unsettling emotions that erupt from somewhere inside of my chest, from some dark pocket behind my eyes. Remembering my own life means knowing that everything can look one way from the outside but there is always another story to be told.

ATLANTA

Uncle Bobby picks me up from the airport in his truck, and I toss my red suitcase into the back before we speed off onto the highway. I am cursing, being grown. Fuck this, goddamn that, shit, you know. "Rebecca the Wrecker," Uncle Bobby calls me, grinning. "You sound like a sailor! Where did you get that mouth?" He slaps my thigh, hard. But then he laughs and shakes his head at me from behind the steering wheel, letting me know he kind of likes it that I am cursing, that I am tough on the outside but sweet on the inside, that I am like him.

When we get to his house my auntie Link is cooking sausage and eggs in the kitchen, her hair in pink and blue spongy rollers as she stands over the sink washing collard greens. The gate slams shut behind me and she turns, looks me over, and tells me I've gotten big. "Come give me a hug," she says, taking me into the warm folds of her gauzy nylon nightgown that smells like bacon, "and some sugar." Uncle Bobby carries my suitcase into my cousins' room, the room I will share with them for the summer. There are dirty football jerseys and Toughskins jeans lying on the floor, pictures of dark-skinned women in bathing suits from *Jet* magazine taped up on the dark wood paneling. The sheets on my bed are blue and white striped, with baseball players on them, little men swinging bats and catching balls.

There are always two televisions going in Uncle Bobby's house, and sometimes the radio on top of that. The TV in his and Auntie Link's bedroom is where we watch *Soul Train, Fat Albert, The James Brown Show,* and soap operas. After I wash my hair behind the plastic pink shower curtain in the downstairs bathroom, I sit on the floor between Auntie Link's legs watching *The Young and the Restless* as she tries to grab my thin brown hair up in cornrows that won't stay because, as my auntie Eva says, "those little curls you got from your daddy keep poking out."

The little TV in the kitchen is where Uncle Bobby and Robbie and Wayne watch football and wrestling and boxing. They bet on who'll win against my cousin Anthony, who is tall and lanky and has a gold front tooth and who lives in the apartment upstairs with the shag carpet and walls covered with Parliament Funkadelic and Rufus album covers. When he comes down they all sit around the table drinking Budweiser, Johnnie Walker Red, and Jack D, my uncle Bobby's favorite.

They sit there late into the night, my uncle with his boys, drinking and shouting and laughing, then growing quiet as it gets later and later, as it reaches three and four A.M. and the whole neighborhood is silent outside of the gate except for the noise of the dogs next door barking when one of the neighbors comes home, his blue Cutlass Supreme bouncing with Funkadelic: "Flashlight, Neon Light," or "One Nation Under a Groove." If I stay up with the boys as Uncle Bobby sometimes lets me do, sitting quietly in my nightgown as the boys talk, I can hear the neighbor's girlfriend open the door for him and ask him where he's been. I hear how he doesn't answer and imagine him pushing by her to get inside, her mother in one of the upstairs bedrooms, pretending to be asleep.

It's not just that the houses are close together, it's that the outside space between the two houses is like an extension of our kitchen and their living room. When people come visit Uncle Bobby, sometimes they stand at the gate for an hour or more, talking through it, or both of them will stand right outside it, on the three little cement steps. We kids hang out in that half-cement half-grass alley all day, watching. I never know the names of the people next door, but I know their business.

I like staying up late because I like the night and because I like to listen and feel grown. Uncle Bobby tells stories about going to Korea in the war and this guy getting cut up on the side of the road downtown and how white people burned my grandfather's store down when they saw he was making money and taking away their business. When we watch boxing he tells stories about Muhammad Ali and Joe Louis, and if James Brown comes on or somebody on the TV says his name, Uncle Bobby reminds us that he's from Augusta and has a big house right over there off that highway we take when we go to visit Granny.

Even though they are boys and even though Uncle Bobby takes me sometimes with him to visit his girlfriend who lives in a trailer on the way to Granny's, my uncles and cousins never talk about women in front of me. It's cars, sports, politics, and money, but no girls, and Uncle Bobby always stops to explain things that I might not understand.

. . .

Uncle Bobby is strict with the boys, but not with me. One day Robbie, my favorite cousin, forgets to put the dogs outside and my uncle Bobby flies into a rage, whipping off his belt and beating both him and his brother Wayne. I am transfixed as I watch him slap them with the brown belt he wears every day and as I watch my big cousins, the ones I look up to, spin around the room in their underwear, trying to avoid the blows. Even though I know my mama told him not to hit me, Uncle Bobby says if I am bad he will. For a few days after that I am afraid of Uncle Bobby, afraid of what his big, rough hands might do. But I am a girl, a daughter not a son, and I know that if I do something bad it is most likely Auntie Link who will punish me, who will tell me to bring her a switch from the yard.

Every four or five days me and Uncle Bobby and Robbie and Wayne and Yadda, the German shepherd, all load up in Uncle Bobby's truck and drive down to the country, to the old shack where my grandmother was born and which my uncles have taken over and filled with freezers full of raw meat, soda, and beer. The Old House is where we have Walker-Lee-Grant Family Reunions every year on the Fourth of July. My uncle Curt makes his famous barbecue sauce and cooks ribs and chicken and fish in a barbecue pit in the backyard. People sit under shade trees in folding chairs by the side of the house and on the screened-in porch, talking, and eating barbecue and cole slaw, potato salad and fresh corn on the cob. We kids run through and around the house, under and between all the grown-ups, playing tag and It, grabbing a chicken leg or a Mountain Dew and being shown off to aunts and uncles and friends of the family who haven't yet seen us but have heard of us, and who we may never see again.

When Granny pulls me over to meet relatives, they all say the same thing, "This here is Alice's baby girl?" And then they look me over carefully, as if to see if I have all ten fingers or maybe a horn growing out of my side somewhere. "Well she sure is, now, ain't she," they say finally. "Sho nuff is Alice's little baby girl, and she's pretty too. She looks just like her mama *and* her daddy." I smile politely, but I can't quite figure this last part out because even though everybody asks after Uncle Mel and tells me to say hello to my daddy for them, I don't remember my daddy ever being here.

The Old House is where Uncle Bobby and Robbie teach me how to use a gun. They take me over to the side of the house in the late afternoon where they have cans on top of sticks, and they put the big heavy metal thing into my hand and tell me to go ahead. I am afraid of the loud noise, of the dull gray thing that can kill so heavy in my hands, but I plant my feet on the ground and I point it out into the woods and I pull on the trigger, getting ready for the kick-back Uncle Bobby says might knock me down. He says it is important that I learn to shoot, that I not be afraid of guns. Sometimes Uncle Bobby carries a gun, in a holster on his hip. With his cowboy boots and gun and baseball hat he looks like one of those guys I see on old movies on television, the ones who walk into the bar and make everybody move out of the way. From Uncle Bobby I learn how to walk like I am tough, like I am not afraid, like I have a gun on my hip.

Sometimes Robbie takes me riding on his motorcycle and we go shrieking through the back roads, me hanging on to his bare waist, screaming as we run over flattened-out snakes and Robbie dares the speed to stop us. Crouched over the handlebars of his old blue Yamaha with the wind flattening his soft dark afro back away from his face, Robbie is becoming a man, and I am loving the way our bodies feel next to each other, the heat and sweat and cold, the way I feel so relaxed and so excited at the same time, the way I know Robbie won't let us crash.

I like being with the boys much better than being with the girls. When my cousin Karla comes to visit wearing a pink dress and shiny black patent leather shoes, Granny says I am rude because I don't want to stay in the house and play with her. She doesn't understand why I always want to go with Uncle Bobby or Uncle Curt, even if they are just riding down the block to Corner Pantry, the convenience store. I don't want to stay in the house, I don't want to watch soap operas or play with dolls, I want to be out riding, out watching my uncles do business, exchanging words with all of the other men they know in town.

When I stay home with Granny, she takes me with her in her big blue car to the Kingdom Hall, where I sit quietly and listen to all of her friends, the Brother so-and-so and the Sister Miss Mary so-and-so, talk and read in serious voices about Jehovah. When we get home she makes me read the little books we buy at the Kingdom Hall, which I don't mind, though I am more interested in collecting the books than reading them. I like the way the smooth cloth covers feel in my hands, I like lining them all up side by side and seeing if I can remember which color goes with what title.

At Uncle Curt's house there are never any books, and there are never any rules either, except that at some point we have to go to bed. Mostly, at Uncle Curt's house, we eat. He stays in the kitchen all day cooking huge pots of crabs, of gumbo, of clams and oysters. Uncle Curt says he is a Cancer, and that is why he likes to eat seafood. Uncle Curt is huge and drives a big white Cadillac he bought to match the one he bought for his wife, my auntie Eva. Their daughter Kietta is my favorite girl cousin because we are almost the same age and we both are quiet, thinking types who aren't afraid of our uncles because they treat us like we are two of the boys. They treat us like we are mature, like we are grown.

One morning after Uncle Curt has come in late from his nightclub, the Blue Flame, he tells me and Kietta to come into his bedroom, where the curtains are drawn shut and the only light is coming from a little lamp he has turned on by the side of his bed. Even though it is dark in the room, we can see that the thick shag carpet is covered with money. Ones, fives, tens, twenties, and hundreds come up to our ankles in his bedroom and our job is to separate them, to make this slushy green paper rug into neat little stacks, each bill pointing the same way.

I have never seen money like this, so much of it splattered across a floor, but I am excited by the idea of it, by the feel and smell of so much money right in front of me, so close to me I can taste it. Uncle Curt still wants to sleep and it is too dark in his room to do the counting and so we carry it out into the living room, which is brighter. On our knees we start to separate the bills, Kietta and I counting ten twenty thirty forty. We flip and count, count and stack until we have separated all of the paper money in Uncle Curt's bedroom. Underneath it we find more, dimes, nickels, and quarters, which Kietta puts carefully into her mechanized piggy bank, dropping one shiny silver piece at a time into the slot. When Uncle Curt wakes up he peels two green rectangles off of the fifties stack and hands them to us, one each. "You two rascals did a good job," he says, patting our heads.

It is at the Old House, too, that I first hear the word *cracker,* but I don't have any idea what it means until ten or fifteen years later, when I am really grown. I don't realize that it is a term black people use for white people, and which signifies the insanity, the cruelty, the maniacal culture of racist white people.

Me and my uncle Bobby, Robbie, and Wayne sit in one of the bedrooms in the Old House, the one that has a big photograph above the bed of my granny standing with all of her sisters from the Kingdom Hall. It is late and we have been shooting and eating and fixing the truck, but now it is dark and we are getting ready for bed by the light of an old kerosene lamp that sits in the bathroom by the jar of peach brandy when it isn't burning. The boys are making jokes and I am laughing hysterically, far more than the jokes call for.

I am intoxicated by the smell and buff and love of these men I adore so, delirious with the airy dampness of the house, the thrill of the gun I have held in my hands, the way I have flown over snakes and pressed my cheek into my cousin's sweaty back. And now it is dark and they are telling ghost stories, and the heady mix of fear and excitement and safety and joy and heat rushes through me and I am full with a giddiness that feels like it is spinning me around in circles. I laugh and laugh in my high-pitched giggle, unable to stop, unable to get control of myself, to calm down, to get into bed and go to sleep.

After twenty minutes or so of this whirlwind, my uncle Bobby says something to the boys that I can't hear, and they start laughing too. What, I say, looking up into his beard wide-eyed in the dark, reaching for his strong arms, What did you say? He turns to me with a grin as wide as my own. I said, Rebecca, that some people would call what you have the "sillies," but we call what you've got the "crackers." And my cousins burst out laughing.

This is a word my uncle Bobby will use again and again to describe me or one of my mannerisms, and my cousins do too, even when I am grown and doing things they think are strange or weird, things they think are not black. Even though they are just kidding and we laugh about it together, a part of me feels pushed away when they say this, like I have something inside of me I know they hate. And so even as we stand there together I am struggling to find my ground, to know where I really belong. How do I reconcile my love for my uncles and cousins with the fact that I remind them of pain?

WASHINGTON, D.C.

At the end of the summer when I am back in Brooklyn, Daddy comes to get me from Mama's house in the old red Volvo. Mama answers the door and invites Daddy inside to sit down, but he just picks up my bags and turns back around. As we load up the car my parents don't hug or look into each other's eyes the way they used to, but seeing them together in one space makes me feel warm and calm, like I don't have to worry, like I can just be myself: Rebecca, Alice and Mel's daughter. I dawdle, move slow, run my fingers over the wooden countertop in the kitchen. I don't want to leave.

But then Daddy says it is time to go, we have to beat the traffic. I hug my mother, wrapping my arms around her waist, pressing my face into the warm, firm pouch of her belly. I don't know how to say goodbye to her, I don't know how to let go of her like this, for months. Shouldn't there be something else we do, some kind of magic trick where she can come inside my body and I can go inside hers? Even though they tell me that I will see Mama in November when she comes to visit me in my new house in Washington, when it is time to drive away, I cry. I cry because I don't want to lose my mama and to go with Daddy feels too much like a choice. Daddy says we are leaving Mama's house and going to his house. It sounds okay when he says the words, like they make sense, but where do I live? Which house is mine?

Once we are on the highway, I settle down next to Daddy in the front seat as he listens to the baseball game on the radio. When he puts his big heavy hand on my thigh and tells me everything will be all right, that he loves me, I lean my head on the fuzzy red headrest and believe him. Staring out the window at the power plants with their big smokestacks along the side of the road, I push all the sad feelings away and let my mind go empty and blank. Taking over for my whole body, my eyes drink in and reflect back out, seeing the huge tanks and factories, but seeing through them too. I don't feel anything that way, I just see, just watch, sitting perfectly still in the car, in between home and a place I don't know, gliding through traffic next to my daddy.

By the time we get to Washington I have pushed the smell and feel of my mother down into a very tight place in the middle of my stomach. Driving up to our new house, I see red brick and green weeds, a tiny path leading to a front door. My stepmother opens the door and I drag my suitcase out of the car, feeling it bump heavy against my thigh. The house is empty and hot and echoes when we talk.

For a second I think I smell my mama's sweet, cherry-brown scent, and I grab at the air with my nose to catch her. I see the maroon and orange quilt on her big wooden bed, the bright red cabinets she painted, the big blue velvet sofa in our living room. The colors in this house are white and brown and beige and an old faded navy blue. The lights are bright, the lamps bare. When my stepmother shows me my room upstairs, the first thing I do is walk over to the window and look outside.

When it is dark and I am walking around the empty house by myself after Daddy and Judy have gone to sleep, I touch everything, trying to make it mine, trying to make it seem real that I am there, in that house now, instead of in my other one. I look at the front door for a long time before climbing up the stairs to my bed. Staring up into the darkness, I feel that I am waiting for something that isn't coming. I am waiting and waiting but I don't know that I am waiting because the feeling is coming from somewhere in my body, somewhere in my stomach and chest and arms and legs and not my head. I am waiting for my mother.

A few nights later when I can't sleep, I find *The Diary of Anne Frank* in my father's bookshelf. It is up on one of the high shelves, next to big thick books with titles I can read but which mean nothing to me. I pull this book down, thinking of the padded red leather diary Grandma gave me, the one with the shiny brass lock. I stare at the picture of the young girl on the cover for a long time, standing on the piano bench I have dragged over to the bookcase. There is something about her eyes that pulls me, that makes me want to know her. I read on the back of the book that she is a young Jewish girl, growing up during World War Two. I take the little book into my room and read it under the covers in my bed, holding the flashlight from the downstairs closet in one hand, pushing the hard sides of the book open with the other.

While I read Anne Frank's diary, I become her. I live in a secret room in a big house, behind a secret door with my family. Sometimes we don't have enough to eat, and sometimes we are afraid we will be caught. I miss my friends and I do everything I can to be helpful and polite, sweet and considerate, even though inside I am lonely and longing to be outside. When I get to the end of the book and read that Anne Frank was taken by the Gestapo and killed, I feel something I have never felt before. I feel terror and loss and like nothing can save me from the same death as Anne's. I imagine the Gestapo is going to come to my house and take me and my father and my stepmother and put us in the back of a truck to Auschwitz. When we get there, big men with guns will separate us, and I will be all alone like Anne was, and I will die just like Anne.

I am certain of this, so certain that my mind goes numb and dark and my bones start to hurt, like someone is pulling at them from the inside, stretching them, making them crack and creak. So certain that when Daddy comes into my room late at night to hold me after I have had yet another nightmare about the Gestapo coming up the stairs and into my room, I don't believe him when he says they can't get us, that the war is over, that we are safe. I don't believe my father when he tells me that he will protect me. I know that the bad people are stronger than him just like they were stronger than Anne's father and that, just like her father couldn't save her, my father won't be able to save me.

In Washington, I live at 644 East Capitol Street, in a red brick row house. My room is at the top of soft blue carpeted stairs, at the back of the house. I have a big double bed and, across from it, a wooden wall unit that holds all of my Nancy Drew books, the little yellow television that Grandma got when she opened a new account at the bank, and my jewelry box. The pine chest of drawers that my stepmother covered with flowery contact paper is next to my bed. On top of it I put the portable yellow and white record player Daddy gave me for my birthday and all of the forty-fives I buy for a dollar fifty at the record store: "I'm Every Woman" by Chaka Khan, "Bustin' Loose" by Chuck Brown and the Soul Searchers, "Car Wash" by Rose Royce.

In Washington my stepmother takes me to school on the first day and walks me to my class even after I lie and tell her that I'll be okay, that I'm not nervous. The truth is that I am not sure I want to be seen with her, I am not sure whether a white mother is going to work for or against me in Washington. Yet every night before bed it is she who makes my lunches, putting the little cans of Welch's grape juice that she knows I like under my bologna sandwich and alongside a Baggie filled with carrot sticks. She who buys me school clothes, dark green velour pullovers and Dijon jeans with satin stripes down the sides. She who crouches down in front of me to look at the hair that starts to grow all thin and fine on my vagina.

And it is she, too, who gets on the phone and finds me a dentist to go to when I have a swollen bump on my gum from all the candy I eat. She walks me to the dentist's office and sits with me in the green and yellow room and talks to the dentist when he says I have an abscess and my tooth will have to come out. She calls me downstairs before dinner, tells me to set the table, teaches me how to make lemon soup, a tossed green salad, salad dressing from vinegar and oil and mustard and freshly ground black pepper. While my father is upstairs sleeping and she is sewing name tags for summer camp on all of my jeans, hooded red sweatshirts, and underwear, it is she, my stepmother, who tells me about penises and vaginas, about how babies are made.

In Washington I don't know what to call her, this woman who mothers me, who introduces herself to salespeople in department stores as my mother even though she is light and white and tall and thin and I am brown and curly-haired; even though sometimes people ask if I am adopted. In New York I called her Judy, Jud, Judith Goldsmith. One day I have some kind of rash and I itch. I call out to her. She is downstairs, in the kitchen. Before I can stop myself I yell out, "Mom, where is the calamine lotion?" And then I stop, resting my hand on the wooden banister, waiting to see if she'll answer me, if she will accept this new name. When she tells me to look in the medicine cabinet in her bathroom, I feel the same feelings I have every time I call her Mom and she answers. I feel giddy and excited, like I am doing something new and fun and dangerous; and I feel duplicitous, shameful, and bad, like I am betraying my mother, like I am choosing this shiny white version over her.

I go to King Elementary School in Washington, and I walk there every day past Machiavelli's Pizza, the record store, and the old theater where I take ballet classes from a woman who tells me I will never be a great ballerina because black women's bodies aren't suited for ballet. She says this one afternoon when we all are at the barre, me and six other little girls. I am wearing the purple and red tie-dye leotard my mama bought me in Brooklyn and all the other little girls are in pink and white. We are learning the jeté, and the girls in front of me are swinging their legs back and forth. When the teacher comes to me she pushes on my belly and tilts my pelvic bone up, so that my tush is pulled toward the floor. You will never get this one hundred percent right, she says out loud. Too much rear end, legs that are not straight. There have never been any famous black ballerinas.

When we turn to face the mirror for pliés, my face burns as I compare my body to the other girls. My thighs are shorter and thicker, my butt is bigger. As we go down I will my legs to turn out like theirs, from the hips and not just at the knee. I contract my muscles with my mind, memorizing the way this feels so I can hold it for the rest of the day and tomorrow, until I no longer need to remember with my mind because my body remembers by itself.

In my fourth-grade class everyone is brown, except a few white kids who come by bus to school. The only other kid who is light like me, not white and not brown either, is Marc. Marc is tall and goofy and has a big forehead and big thick glasses. Walking through the hallways between classes and out in the playground at recess, the other kids make fun of Marc, and sometimes they punch him in the arm so hard he wants to cry but can't because he knows they will hit him harder if he does, they will call him crybaby and sissy. As it is they say he is mellow-yellow and blind as a bat, even though he is not the only one in the class who wears glasses.

In school I don't talk to Marc, I am too afraid that the other kids will see that I am like him, yellow and awkward and afraid instead of cool and tough like I pretend to be. But I do talk to him after school, when we are walking home and I see him walking the same way as me, but across the street like he is scared to get too close. All year Marc lets me be his sometimes, after-school friend, as if we have made a secret pact. In school when the kids tease him I turn away from his face when he is about to cry, even though I feel sorry for him, even though I know how lonely and afraid he is. After school I trail along next to him, our backpacks rubbing against our shoulder blades. We look at trees together and talk about the ones we like. We especially notice when there is one missing in the sidewalk, a pole with a parking sign stuck into the cement where a tall leafy green thing should be.

Malaika Pierce is my best friend. Malaika is short and brown, with plaits on either side of her head, a big toothy smile, and two big dimples. Malaika is sweet like chocolate, Malaika is innocent like milk, Malaika is always making jokes, always standing by my side, Malaika is my best friend. She is the friend I don't worry about, the friend I trust, the friend who is so close I don't tell her my secrets because I think she must know them already, and besides, when we are together everything and everyone else is irrelevant.

Malaika is my best friend like Karen was, but better because we go to the same school and spend the night at each other's houses two or three times a week. We are like sisters but also not because we don't fight, we don't compete for our parents' attention. My father is always working and her mother is too and so most of the time we are in our own little world, a world without parents, where mainly we have just each other. At school Malaika takes care of me when the fifth- and sixth-grade black girls tell me I'm too white or that I am weak and a coward because I don't want to fight them or that I am acting like I think I know everything.

We'll be in the yard at recess and those girls will stand over by the jungle gym saying things and Malaika will go to the guy on the corner and buy us both two big sour kosher pickles, handing me one and turning her back to those girls named Deanna and Simone, those girls I never did anything to, those girls I don't know and who don't know me, those girls who never look happy, who never look clean, who never look cared for.

When we go back and forth between our houses, Malaika's mother, Patricia, drives us in her little car. I am fascinated by the big plastic key chain that dangles from the ignition. It spells her name in big white letters that you can feel when you run your fingers over them. For most of the year that Malaika and I are best friends, she doesn't meet my mother and I don't meet her father. Sometimes she mentions him, but he seems like a shadow I can't make out, even though I squint my eyes when Malaika talks about him in his house in South Carolina or wherever it is he lives. Trying to see, I ask her, Do you look like him? and then I help her change the subject after she is quiet, after she can't figure out how to answer the question.

We are like sisters but I want to sleep naked next to Malaika, I like the warmth of our bodies flush against each other under the cool cotton of the blue sheets my stepmother puts on the bed for us in the guest room. In the dark there we twist this way and that, sometimes sweating from all of our rubbing. I like the color of Malaika's body, I like how brown she is, like Mama. When I look at her I feel the deep brown of her skin pour into me through my eyes and fill me up in a place that feels cold and empty, a place that I forget I have until I look at her naked body.

On nights when I can convince her, Malaika plays Daddy and

I play Mommy. I want to be the one who is touched more, the one who is done to, the one who is told what to do. Some nights we play with one of my father's old leather belts. I like the sound of it slapping my skin, the warm heat I feel when Malaika hits me, when Malaika plays Daddy.

This year, in this school, the play is *Grease,* and I want more than anything to be in it. I want to sit after school in the empty auditorium with the other students singing along to the words of all my favorite *Grease* songs and wearing the black leather jackets and yellow hoop skirts that I see in the costume box. Every day after school for a week I go to the auditorium and sit there, trying to find my way into the process of casting and putting on this show, but I can't figure out how to get past the tough black girls who seem to have taken the whole thing over and who sneer at me from the stage, laughing every time I say I want to be Rizzo, the tough girl who thinks she is pregnant and who everybody calls a slut.

When my stepmother asks why I am not in the school play, I tell her it is because of the girls who hate me for no reason. I tell her I am afraid of them, I am afraid of what they will do to me if I speak too loud, if I say too loud that I want to play Rizzo and dance around on stage in the lines with all of the other girls and boys, singing words I already know by heart. When my stepmother comes to speak up for me to the teachers, to the people who are running the show, she sits quietly in the auditorium for a while first, trying to understand what is happening, trying to make out who is in charge.

But it is just like I told her, and she sees that a thin girl named Felicia is running the show and that she has all the other girls, and some of the boys too, helpless in her thrall. Teachers walk through the space, short blondish women who talk to each other and don't look at the stage as they cross from one side of the big auditorium to the other. They don't want to see that they are not in charge, that they too are afraid of black girls half their size, a quarter of their age, black girls who are hardened and angry and don't have a lot to lose.

Sitting with my stepmother on the plastic folding chairs facing the stage, I don't see that if I want to be inside I must pay a price, like the teachers and all the other girls. I don't understand that to be in this play I have to make myself smaller, tiny even, so that I won't threaten anyone else, so that I won't make the one in charge feel pain that she will turn into anger. What I see is all the other girls in the place that I want to be, all the other girls feeling what it feels like to be inside, not alone, not strange, alien, other.

There is a pain in my chest as I watch the girls. I think, there must be something wrong with me, I am too clunky, too big, not graceful. Not black enough. When I think these thoughts I think them quickly, so fast I do not even know they are there, so fast they do not register in my mind but take hold somewhere in my body, somewhere in my soul. Instead of saying, I hate those girls and I want to kill them, I say, I am not good at acting. Instead of asking her to make it stop, to make them accept me, I tell my stepmother, I didn't really want to do that anyway.

When Mama comes to pick me up for the weekend it is already dark, and I am upstairs watching *Charlie's Angels*, my favorite television show. On the floor in front of my yellow television set I have laid out all my *Charlie's Angels* cards, and when my baby-sitter calls upstairs that my mother is waiting, I make one last frantic attempt to make all the rectangular puzzle pieces fit into the one picture of three women holding guns. I haven't seen Mama since the summer, and a lot has happened. I have started to grow hair on my vagina. I have a new best friend named Malaika Pierce. I call my stepmother Mom.

Mama is waiting for me on the skinny brick walkway leading up to the door. She is wearing her black winter coat, and when I come out she gives me a big hug and takes my hand, asking me if I have everything I will need for the weekend away. Do I have clean underwear? Do I have a sweater? Mama is wearing the sharp musky perfume she always wears, the black pants with a zipper in the back I remember from when we lived on Garfield, but she looks different, older, cold.

I want Mama to come inside and see my room: the new fold-up record player with the little pocket that holds forty-fives, the tree outside my window, my jewelry box. I don't say anything because I don't know how, I don't know how to say, "Mama, I want," and besides, Mama is already walking fast, pulling me along with her away from the house and onto the sidewalk. She doesn't look back as the heels of her boots click click against the cement and I have already forgotten my wish, so busy am I trying to keep up, trying to keep up with my mama.

When I climb into the backseat of the car across the street, it is like I am entering another world, a world I know my father and stepmother and baby-sitter can never enter. It is a world of politics and poetry, small cars, Indian restaurants, and curvy brown and beige women who are larger than life. Stevie Wonder is singing "Isn't She Lovely" on the tape player as I sit on the red vinyl seat next to my mama, and she hands me a package wrapped in tissue paper. Inside the fuchsia paper is a white linen shirt, dashiki-style but without the colors, and a necklace made of shells.

When I put the presents that Mama has given me on over my shoulders, I feel more prepared for where we are going, for my weekend life with Mama and her friends. When we drive away from the house, I don't watch it disappear out the back window. I am too busy being looked at by my mama, being stroked and held, talked at and listened to. I sit, trying to let my body open up again like it was when Mama and I lived together, trying to let it get warm again after being so cold.

.   .   .

M ama and I stay with a lawyer friend of hers who lives on the top floor of a house in Georgetown. The ceilings are slanted, straw curtains separate the bedroom from the living room, and there is a bathtub in the kitchen under a board. In this woman's house there is incense burning and sweet-smelling, beautiful black women in flowing dresses of African print who laugh and discuss racism, sexism, and imperialism late into the night. The women burn candles, order in Chinese food, and spread out red, blue, and purple scarves on the table in the living room to read tarot cards. In between readings they talk about law and transcendental meditation and women they know who are traveling around the world.

Before I go to bed they add up all the numbers in my birthday and tell me I am a seven, the most spiritual number. These women are singers, and they rehearse one of their songs while sitting around the table, all their voices mixing and melting into a lullaby that puts me to sleep behind the bamboo curtain. They are called Sweet Honey in the Rock, and when my mother reads at the Library of Congress, they sing too.

At the Library of Congress, I become the daughter of my mother. That is how people know me, that is what I am called, over and over. This is Alice's daughter, this is Alice's little girl. This is the speaker's daughter. This is Alice Walker's daughter. You know that woman who read the poetry? This is her daughter. It is easy to be my mama's daughter, all I have to do is stand next to her and smile at all the people who come over to talk and shake her hand. The people are all different, they are older black women carrying bags full of books, they are polite white men with glasses and cream-colored sweaters, they are shy Japanese college students who nod their heads from a distance instead of asking Mama for her hand to shake, they are older black men with cameras who want to take a picture of me and Mama together, in front of the table full of books.

I do not mind being my mother's daughter, I like it even. I like the attention, the way the people who love my mother's writing dote on me and make me feel like I am special, too. Standing by my mother's elbow at the head of the long line of people, I make myself available to them and drink in all of their adoration. They want to touch my mother, but mostly they want to look at me, to search my face for signs of her. Do I write? What do I want to be when I grow up? Am I proud of my mama? I write sometimes, I say, I want to be a lawyer like my daddy, I say. Am I proud of my mother? This question is harder to answer. I am not sure I understand the emotion they are looking for, not sure I am supposed to be proud of my mother. Isn't she supposed to be proud of me?

When Mama leaves the next morning, waving to me from the backseat of an old white and blue taxi, life snaps back to the way it was before she came. My stepmother makes my lunches and my daddy goes to work. I go to ballet class and walk with Marc home from school. No one says anything about being my mother's daughter.

SAN FRANCISCO

B ethany and I go to the little school on the rooftop of Raphael Weill, the huge public elementary school with the bad reputation. Our school is called New Traditions Center. We call it NTC. NTC is a hippie school, but we kids don't know that, we know only that it is "alternative." At NTC we skip, we don't run, at playtime. We do Tai Chi at recess. We sit in our classes in a circle on the floor. We have rabbits in cages, we have iceplant and cactus growing in long wooden boxes. We do exercises with long ribbons on the ends of sticks. We sew puffy quilted squares that hang in the hallway. We learn "Norwegian Wood" from a guy with long hair and glasses who looks like he wants to be in the Beatles.

At NTC, when we get into trouble we have to go sit alone in a closet with a colored mat on the floor and a curtain where the door is supposed to be. Each classroom has one, a Quiet Area, and when you're too loud or if you do something disruptive one of our teachers, Frances or Joshua or Alan, we call them by their first names, tells you, Rebecca or Jomo or Sunlight or River or Nile or

Ivan, you need to go visit the Quiet Area until you calm down, or until you can be a better class participant.

Bethany is my best friend and Dakeba is my boyfriend, until Dakeba is Bethany's boyfriend, then everything changes. But first, in the beginning, Dakeba is my boyfriend and Jomo is Bethany's boyfriend. I bring my mother's boyfriend's Panasonic cassette player to school every day and at lunch we build this thing called the clubhouse out of big blocks on the roof and only we four are allowed inside. We kiss there, our backs and legs pressed against the cool, slick concrete, Dakeba and Jomo all heavy on top of me and Bethany, pushing their tongues into our mouths. We play Michael Jackson's *Off the Wall* over and over.

Then after Christmas break everything changes and Dakeba tells me that he and Bethany are going out. Then one day Robert, the retarded kid in our class, pushes me out the heavy metal downstairs door onto the street. Robert is bigger than me, blacker, with messed-up crooked teeth that are green at the gum and cross-eyes that are always filled with gunk. Every day he wears the same black knit hat and navy blue bomber jacket. Brown corduroys with filthy cuffs hang down below his waist, showing the blue and red stripes on the elastic of his underwear. On some days the underwear inches down and you can see the crack of Robert's butt.

When Robert pushes me out the door I feel the metal of the bars cut hard into my back. From the other side of the door, the outside side, I think about running into one of the yellow school buses waiting there, but I don't know where those buses go and my name isn't on the bus list and my house is just a couple of blocks away. San Francisco Unified School District, the bus says, and I look back at Robert looking at me, pushing me now onto the side street, onto the patch of cement in front of a parking lot which is about to become our battleground.

Dakeba comes charging out of the building. He shouts to Robert, Get her! And then Robert stands in front of me and won't let me by and starts pushing me with big, rough ashy hands. Dakeba gets behind me and when Robert pushes me my back slams into his chest. When Dakeba pushes me back, my chest shoves into Robert's. Mostly I feel ribs, theirs and mine hitting against each other. In the distance I can see the walkway to my house. I know my mother is home. In my mind's eye I can see her in the kitchen. Then they stop pushing and Robert punches me in my stomach. "You scared now, you should be." He kicks me. I struggle but Dakeba holds me still. I ask them why they are doing this and Dakeba says, It doesn't matter why, you yellow bitch.

I'm in San Francisco and it's different. There are hills and blue skies and fog that comes rolling in around five o'clock and doesn't burn off in the mornings until ten or eleven. We live in a little apartment, me and my mom, and her boyfriend Robert comes over sometimes to see us for dinner and sometimes to spend the night. I talk to my father once every couple of months. He's never been where I live so he can't picture it, and he doesn't try. He doesn't ask me what it's like, he doesn't ask for details so that I can tell he's trying to get a picture of it in his mind. When he calls and I tell him about what we do here in San Francisco, like go to the hot tubs to soak or to Double Rainbow on Polk Street for ice cream or to the Japanese restaurant for miso soup or to the women's bookstore where Mama gives readings, he says really but he sounds like he's a million miles away. He's never even been to California.

I don't tell him about Dakeba or about people calling me yellow or about being hit. I keep all that inside and try to sound happy when he calls, or tough, like I am handling everything, like the world Mama lives in is perfect. And sometimes it is, like when Mama and I lie in her big bed in the evening watching *Soap* or *Upstairs, Downstairs* on television, or when I sit in my bedroom cutting out pictures from magazines and taping them to my bedroom closet, or when I am reading *A Hero Ain't Nothing but a Sandwich* by Alice Childress, or *Sunshine* by Norma Klein, about the woman who has a baby and then finds out she has cancer and only so many months to live.

B ethany's mother lives in a trailer in a field outside of the city. Bethany and I go there after school one Friday afternoon, riding in the back of one of the SamTrans buses out past Orinda. I have twenty dollars that Mama left me pressed into the back pocket of my jeans. Bethany, I'm sure because she never has any money, has less than that.

Once we sit down in our seats, Bethany pushes open the big window, sliding the sheet of glass until the tips of her straight brown hair get caught in the wind and go flat against the outside of the pane. I rummage through our makeup bag as she stares out at the exhaust rising into the dried-up hills. The bag is full of pink and green mascara wands, brownish red squares of blush tucked beside tiny white-handled brushes, and lip gloss, the sticky, shiny, roll-on kind that comes in flavors like Popsicles: grape, strawberry, cola. I put on some cola, licking my lips slightly for the taste, trying to get just enough for the sweetness but not too much because then it tastes like glue.

After a couple of hours down the straightaway and an hour or so on a road so windy and narrow I am afraid the bus might flip, we pull up at our stop, some name I can't pronounce and that I don't let stick into my head. We lower ourselves off the bus, two city girls in jeans and high-tops, big fifth-graders with boyfriends back at school, and stand in the middle of nowhere, brown fields of dried-up dirt stretching endlessly on either side.

After the bus pulls away, Bethany's mother drives up out of nowhere onto the shoulder at the edge of the road in a faded beige Dodge Dart she says belongs to her boyfriend. Rick? Bethany asks as I throw my bag into the car and squish in the middle. Sammy, her mother says, and then Bethany rolls her eyes and sucks her teeth.

The car smells like clean laundry and rides low to the ground, like one of the cholo cars we see all the time on Mission Street, Bethany and me, the boys behind the wheels covered with tattoos and hair nets. When they pass they don't look at me, light brown and awkward with no body to speak of, but Bethany, with her skintight Lees and gauzy shirts, gets it every time. They pop their cars up and down as we cross the street in front of the big stands full of fruit, underneath the signs that say *Sandía* and *Melón* and *Coco* in yellow cursive. Then they yell out at her: *Blanca, blanca, ven aquí.* Come here, white girl.

Bethany, with all her tough walking and showy clothes, is skittish, scared, shy. She looks at her feet, long brown eyelashes fluttering downward as her Converse high-tops hit the asphalt in careful, measured steps. I look at the boys when they call out, staring right in their eyes to see the way they look at Bethany, with that angry hunger. But looking back is against the rules. Bethany gets come here, and I get what the fuck you looking at, *morena*?

W hy do you look like such a fucking slut, Bethany's mother asks after we've been driving a few minutes. All that eye makeup, Jesus. What did you do, rob a fucking drugstore? That eyeliner. Your grandmother lets you wear that shit? Never in a million years would she have let me wear that when I was your age. She's slow-moving, Bethany's mom, weary, with a weathered, angular face, pale but for a swath of dark pink for a mouth. She seems tired and used-up and rock-hard inside. But then something soft comes through, something I don't expect, and it catches me off guard because her body and her face don't look like they would ever be soft, the way she is holding tight to the steering wheel, turned away from the two of us while she is driving, like she doesn't really want us there but tolerates us.

She says, Hey, cookie, I've missed you, and Hey, what do you kids want for dinner because I've got some tofu burgers and not a whole lot else, but I have a few bucks and I know your grandma didn't send you here with no money so we can go get some food from a diner I know. If that's what you kids want.

We pull up to the trailer, a big silvery thing way off the road, sitting up on blocks with nothing else around it but tall grass, with barely a path leading up to it. Inside, there is a tiny kitchen right when you walk in, a butcher-block countertop with little plastic Baggies filled with herbs and cornmeal and oatmeal. The color of the light in the trailer is that magic-hour gold, a color that always reminds me of Bethany even after we stop being friends and I run into her on Haight Street when she is a skinhead and has a swastika painted on her scalp and is wearing a tartan skirt and a military jacket and is so pale I can hardly recognize her and probably wouldn't have if it weren't for her green eyes and long eyelashes. And the way she walked that was so familiar to me, in those careful, fragile little steps.

I am so happy to see her after three or four years that I stop on Haight Street, the street we walked up and down when we were kids, younger, in fifth grade, and I cry, seeing her, reaching out to her, to this shell of someone I knew. But she holds herself back, looking at me but looking away too, at a dirty skinhead boy standing in front of Reckless Records. There is a huge safety pin holding her skirt closed, and she has a scratch on her face, which is blotchy and red. I can tell she is nervous, stuck in something she doesn't know how to get out of.

I ignore him, the angry-looking boy, and try to pull her into me with my eyes, to say, Hey, what's going on, how is your grandmother and do you remember when we went to visit your mother out in wherever the fuck that was?

But Bethany doesn't stand in front of me for long enough to say all of those things. I hug her and then I see the big orange 43 Masonic bus pull up to the stop in front of the bagel store and I see the boy beckon out of the corner of my eye and then Bethany is slipping away from me again, gone. And I am back on Haight Street alone again, walking, as if she had never been there.

There is a big mattress in the back of the trailer, under the back window, which is propped open with a stick. I look at that bed and think about Bethany's mom sleeping there with Rick and Sammy. I imagine her naked, brown hair all mussed up, leaning over the side of the bed to light a cigarette, a Lucky Strike or a Camel. It all is messy, the bed, blankets and pillows and sheets tangled up into ropes. Clothes all over the floor. The bathroom is in between the kitchen and the back, a green plastic toilet seat over a hole that flushes with a rusted foot pedal.

Bethany goes through the kitchen methodically, like she's been doing this every day for all of her eleven or twelve years, checking to see what her mother has, how bad it is. There are food stamps in the single drawer, a lone Tupperware container on the top shelf of the fridge. In a cabinet above the sink there is a half-full box of cereal that Bethany shakes up and down.

When the inspection is over, Bethany pulls some green bills, real money and not the light brown and blue government coupons her mother has, out of her pocket. She waves it in the air for a few seconds, to get her mother's attention. It's from Grandma, she says, and picks up her mother's bag, a straw thing with a taped broken handle, and puts the money inside. Relief floods her mother's face, and I watch as the lines around her eyes and on the sides of her mouth disappear, as she relaxes, finally, into the room.

That night we go to sleep under a sky so dark we can't see each other. It is cold, northern California cold, desert cold, and Bethany and I lie next to each other under old colorful Mexican blankets her Mom scrounges from her bed and the trunk of the Dart. We can hear her mother and Sammy inside the trailer, talking loud in long loopy sentences that roll one right after the other. We can't make out what they are saying and we don't try. We are too busy staring into the darkness and waiting for our eyes to adjust, to make it so that we aren't just our senses, not just the smell of minerals coming up out of the earth and the sound of crickets, but real girls with solid bodies and our own free will.

We wake up just after sunrise the next morning, damp, to the sounds of Bethany's mother packing the car. She is dragging blankets and bags past our sleeping bags like she is in some kind of huge hurry to get somewhere. We're going to the city, she says, sounding at once completely focused and a million miles away. I've got to get you girls back.

Afrer their divorce is final and they sell the house we all three lived in, and after my father takes a government civil rights job in Washington, D.C., and my mother moves to San Francisco where she feels she can write better because she can see the sky, my parents decide that I will spend two years, alternately, with each of them. I don't know how they come up with that number, two, as opposed to one, or why they didn't simply put me in junior high here and high school there. I don't know if staying in one city so that I wouldn't have to spend my life zigzagging the country, so that I could have some semblance of a normal relationship with friends and family members, ever crossed either of my parents' minds.

What their decision means is that every year of my life I have to move, change schools, shift. My father returns to the life that was expected of him, marrying a nice Jewish girl he met as a kid in summer camp, and my mother falls for a Morehouse man, an old sweetheart from her Spelman days. For them there is a return to what is familiar, safe, expected. For me there is a turning away from all of those things.

Now as I move from place to place, from Jewish to black, from D.C. to San Francisco, from status quo middle class to radical artist bohemia, it is less like jumping from station to station on the same radio dial and more like moving from planet to planet between universes that never overlap. I move through days, weeks, people, places, growing attached and then letting go, meeting people and then saying goodbye. Holding on makes it harder to be adaptable, harder to meet the demands of a new place. It is easier to forget, to wipe the slate clean, to watch the world go by like a film on a screen, without letting anything stick.

wo-piece, extra biscuit two-piece, extr
iscuit two-piece, extra biscuit two
iece, extra biscuit two-piece, extra bis
uit two-piece, extra biscuit two-piece
xtra biscuit two-piece, extra biscuit two
iece, extra biscuit two-piece, extra bis
uit two-piece, extra biscuit two-piece
xtra biscuit two-piece, extra biscuit two
ece, extra biscuit two-piece, extra bis
uit two-piece, extra biscuit two-piece
tra biscuit two-piece, extra biscuit two
ece, extra biscuit two-piece, extra bis
it two-piece, extra biscuit two-piece
tra biscuit two-piece, extra biscuit two
ece, extra biscuit two-piece, extra bis
it two-piece, extra biscuit two-piece
tra biscuit two-piece, extra biscuit two
ece, extra biscuit two-piece, extra bis
it two-piece, extra biscuit two-piece

Asha is Colleen's little sister. She walks into Colleen's room from the hallway between Colleen's room and the bathroom. The bathroom is brown and yellow, everything in it covered with cut-out pieces of fuzzy carpet. Asha has on a frilly light blue and pale pink dress with matching bows in her hair, plastic birdie barrettes swinging from each braid. When she comes by me I can smell grease in her hair, green Afro-Sheen, can see her shiny, yellow scalp. Asha's eyes are green, which makes her cute, everyone talks about Asha's eyes a lot: that they are green, that they are pretty.

I'm sitting in Colleen's bedroom, uncomfortable on her canopy bed, my bare legs scratching against the nylon ticking in the bedspread. She's playing Prince. "I Wanna Be Your Lover." I've never heard of Prince. There's a poster of him behind me, over the bed. He's in the shower, with only a little bikini bathing suit on. *I ain't got no money. I ain't like those other guys you hang around.* There are suds running down his body. His tongue is out. Colleen's mother comes in and tells her, "Turn that music down, turn that freak music down." Colleen's mother works at the post

office, every day she goes there and weighs and stamps. When
Mama sends me for stamps, Colleen's mother, Mrs. Braxton, I call
her, helps me. She tears the little squares off in strips and puts
them in big envelopes made of wax.

Colleen is a friend of Michael's, the boy I met while I was
baby-sitting the twins. The twins are Saul and Liana and they are
black and Jewish like me, but we never talk about that. It's a non-
issue, something that isn't in the conversation, like what school
you go to or where your father works. We never say, like, Hey, I'm
black and Jewish too, what's that about for you? We never say, Isn't
it strange when . . . We're just black when people want to claim us
and weird when they don't. The twins live with their mother, she's
Jewish, across the square from me. They are only a couple of years
younger than I am, but my mother says I should make some extra
money and so I baby-sit them. Sometimes I play basketball with
them in the second square, and that's how I meet Michael.

I am wearing my green tee shirt and the jeans that Judy
bought me with the satin stripes up the side. The twins are trying
to get the ball from me, and because I am only a little taller than
they are, they are succeeding. Michael rides by on his ten-speed
bike, the one with the curled-down handlebars. It is blue. He is
wearing an orange shirt that flashes against his dark brown skin.
He is so fine to me that it scares me. He rides by and looks at me
and then he rides by again and looks at me some more. I look back
the second time. The third time he circles me and the twins and
then stops and asks me some questions. "You from around here?"
he says. I say no and yes. He asks me where I am from. I tell him
New York, Washington, D.C., Mississippi.

He asks how old I am. I lie. I say fifteen. I pretend like I know what I am doing, talking to this cute fine sexy boy older than me, but I don't know what I am doing. I don't know how to hold my body, when to breathe, if I should look at him when we talk. I don't know if being myself is enough. I don't think it is.

That night I ask my mama for a bike. I want one because I want to ride around the square like Michael. She says no, and to ask my grandma for money for it. I call my grandma in Brooklyn and she says yes, she will send me the money and she does and so one day I go with my mother's boyfriend to Sears to buy my ten-speed bike. I feel strange going in there to buy it, because I have the money and there are so many bikes and it is all on me to do. I am not sure I am doing the right thing, picking the red one, but I do it anyway. They bring me there and tell me to pick it out and so I pick a red one and we put it into our little car and bring it home.

When I'm not riding my bike, I keep it in the walk-in closet with the TV. Every time you go into the closet to get the TV, you have to move my bike from resting on it and put it against the wall. After a few months of me hauling the bike up and down the stairs, the hallway in our building has skid marks on the floor from my bike. The walls, too, from where the wheels hit when I carry it up the three flights.

I don't see Michael again until a few weeks later when I am riding my bike. I stop in the square with the basketball court, where I had the twins, where I met Michael that first time. I stop at that bench to catch my breath a minute, resting my bike against the chess table. I don't do all of that in one smooth motion. I am awkward. I slow the bike to a stop, skinning my shin against the bench. I climb off the bike and turn the handle bars the way I hope will move the thing to the right when I back it up. It moves to the left so I turn the bars the other way. Then I lean it against the table. It falls down. I bend down, pick it up, prop it better, and then sit down. It falls down again.

Two girls, Sonja and Sandra, come down from the building up the hill, the one that has the window in it that Michael was watching that day when I met him. Sonja is big. I don't know it then but everyone in her family is big, strong, meaty. She has her hair in plaits and has on these big burgundy overalls with jelly shoes and pom-pom socks. The pom-poms are yellow and blue, she must have on two pairs, one over the other. I don't remember Sandra too much, not her skin or her hair or anything in particular. Sonja is the one who tells me she is going to take my bike from me. Sonja is the one who asks me where am I from and am I new and says she should just take my bike so I could learn what it is like. I say, What *what* is like?

Then Michael comes up to where we all three are sitting, on that bench. And he sees them, what they are doing, and he tells them to stop. He says, Come on, y'all don't have nothing better to do than bother this girl? Y'all are too old to be doing this. What are you, Sonja, sixteen, with a baby up in the house. Y'all need to stop. And then he looks at me. He doesn't say are you all right or anything corny like that either. He just looks at me. He doesn't smile because he knows that would make those girls even more mad than they already are. He just looks at me and then he sits down and starts talking shit with those two girls.

I don't leave because I don't want them to think I am afraid of them and also I don't know what the right thing is to do and also

I don't want to leave Michael and so I just stay, and watch as Michael unwraps his body onto the bench and jokes around with those girls. After a while I start to breathe again.

C olleen puts "Lady Cab Driver" on the stereo. She just moves the needle to that song and it starts to play: *Lady cab driver, can I take you for a ride.* In the song Prince is in New York, and I know New York, I know about cabs and cab drivers because I have lived there, and Colleen has not. To her it is a place that is far, alien, cool, scary. When Colleen and Michael talk about New York, when they ask me what it is like, they ask if it is true that everyone is always getting robbed and can you walk out on the streets alone. I say it is tough, because it is, but that no, it isn't that bad. They look at me different when I say that, when they see that I can talk about New York with knowledge, that it is my city too, like San Francisco is for them, like it is going to be for me.

Colleen asks me if I like Michael. She says, He's cute, huh? I say, Yeah, but I don't know him that well and I have a boyfriend. She says, real surprised, You have a boyfriend? I say, Yeah, don't you? Asha keeps walking in and out of Colleen's room where we're sitting and talking. She looks like a little doll, but she doesn't move stiff like that, she moves like she wants to play, like she's rolling herself to one side and then the other, like she's roller-skating. Asha is younger than me, but I am younger than Colleen. It's awkward, being in the middle like that. When Colleen tells Asha to go get a comb so she can do her hair, I want her to say the same thing to me. I want Colleen to say, "Go get a comb and bring it to me so that I can do your hair." I want to be on the floor like that, like Asha eventually is, between Colleen's legs, in the warm there, knowing my place, knowing what to do.

The things about Colleen that make me nervous are that she's older than me and she has curves. She has big breasts and round hips and gold rings and necklaces and she wears lipstick and everything about her is Girl. She also has this attitude, like when Michael asks her something that isn't his business, like who her man is, she answers back, Get out of here, shit, why don't you leave me alone. Or, That ain't none of your business. Colleen can stick up for herself. She's a real black girl, and I'm not. When someone asks me something like that, or makes a joke about what I have on or the way I talk, I answer straight, directly. I'm too serious, too stiff to hit the ball back, to bounce some words across the pavement. They say I'm more like a white girl.

Also Colleen goes to Sacred Heart. She wears a blue school uniform with a red bow at the neck, and so does her little sister Asha. I am jealous of their uniform, the way it makes them stand out from everyone else, the way it matches them to each other, the way it says to the world that they are together instead of separate. I imagine Colleen and Asha and their mother going to the store where they sell uniforms and buying all of the pieces together: the socks, the shoes, the little red tie that goes around their necks. The little pleated skirt and gold pin that says Sacred Heart. When I go to school I wear one of three pairs of pants: my jeans, my olive green Calvin Klein corduroys, or the turquoise Gloria Vanderbilts I bought with Faith on sale at Macy's.

Faith is the woman my mother hires to take me clothes shopping for school. My mother says she is too busy to do it, too tired.

She gives Faith her Macy's card with a note saying that Faith is authorized to use it. She types the letter on her typewriter and signs it with a blue felt-tipped pen. We are allowed to spend eighty dollars on school clothes and that isn't very much so we spend a lot of time in the sale section, looking through the racks, trying to find things that are good but also cheap. We find one flowery shirt and the Gloria Vanderbilt pants and a gray sweater.

Faith is fine. She takes me on the 38 Geary bus, and she does the shopping with me and then she brings me home on the 38 Geary bus and then she rings the buzzer and brings me back upstairs and then my mother gives her some money, twenty dollars, and then she says goodbye and then she leaves. I don't see her again.

After Faith comes Danita. Danita lives downstairs from me with her mother, Vondie. Vondie has some kind of corporate job and so her house is like that: corporate. She has burgundy and cream everything. Rug, blinds, place mats for the glass table. Burgundy and cream towels in the bathroom. Even her car is burgundy, a Cutlass Supreme with plush interior. Danita and Vondie have two big televisions, one in the living room and one in the back, in Vondie's burgundy and cream bedroom. Both televisions are always on.

When I see Vondie at home through a crack in her door, she is in bed with reading glasses on, leafing through junk mail and catalogues. When I see her going to work I don't recognize her. She has on high heels and a business blazer with a silky scarf billowing from around her neck and big fake gold earrings. Vondie unwinds at the end of the day in her bedroom with the blinds pulled, sipping on a cocktail. Sometimes when my mother is away and Danita is looking out for me, I go downstairs into their dark apartment to watch *Soul Train*. Danita makes eggs and bacon and asks me if she should make me a plate. I always say yes.

My house is pretty empty compared to Danita and Vondie's, "not cluttered," my mother would say, with greenish-yellow carpet. There is a sliding glass door in the living room to the little terrace where my mother has plants: jade, petunias, some kind of little flowering vine. When my mother is away my refrigerator is empty. So empty that when I ask Michael to come upstairs, he looks inside and says, "Damn, you don't have no food." I don't say anything, but I feel embarrassed, like I am naked, or maybe poor. Michael after that makes jokes about how empty my refrigerator is. He tells people, people who are his age, who were his friends before I met them, people like Colleen and Tony and Mark, that there isn't ever anything in my house to eat. "They don't even have no guv'ment cheese," he says.

On the nights I don't eat with Danita, driving in the Cutlass Supreme to the soul food place on Hayes or to the burrito place in the Mission, I go to Kentucky Fried Chicken for a two-piece, extra biscuit. I say that to myself as I walk the three blocks to the place, Two-piece, extra biscuit, rehearsing for the moment when I will walk up to the counter.

Michael and I kiss for the first time in front of the laundry room after I put the clothes in the dryer. I am wearing my faded stonewashed jeans and jelly shoes and my mother's red hooded sweatshirt with the zipper down the front. I walk out of the washroom after putting the clothes in the dryer, and I see him, out of the corner of my eye on his bike, flying down the hill, sitting back in the seat, legs holding the pedals just tight enough to coast. I want him to see me but I don't want to look like I want him to, and so I sit down on one of the logs sticking up out of the sand in the playground outside of the washroom, and I look in his direction but pretend to be looking past him. He keeps coming until he is in front of me and then he stops in front of me just like I want him to, straddles his bike, puts his feet flat on the ground. Hey, he says, not out of breath, cool. I'm happy to see you. I nod. You doin' laundry? Nod, nod, nod.

We say a few other things I don't remember, but my heart is beating really fast when he says happy to see you, and I remember the inside of my thighs brushing the rubber of his front wheel, and then leaning in and smelling him through his blue Polo shirt. He is wearing some kind of cologne and the smell of it is mixed with soap. And then his mouth is on mine and my tongue is inside his mouth and both our tongues are moving around and I feel like I am falling inside of him, like all the stuff around me is gone and my stomach starts doing something too. Something I have never felt before, fluttering, like there is some kind of winged creature in there, trying to get out. It's different from Dakeba, different from anything I have ever felt because this is Michael, this boy who is older and fine and followed me and protected me and makes me feel grown and womanly. He doesn't want to kiss in a clubhouse, he wants to come over to my house when my mother is away.

Weeks later he asks me. We are on the phone. A man from Pacific Bell came and installed a red Trimline on the wall by my closet for my birthday and that's what I talk to Michael on. The cord is long and reaches into my bed and out onto the fire escape that is on the other side of the little door by my bookshelves. It is late at night and I am whispering so that my mama won't hear. It is hot and I have the fire-escape door open. He is talking all sweet. Pleading with me. Can I come over? Then he lowers his voice. C'mon, lemme come over. I just want to see you and talk to you in person. I look out at all the other buildings, all the other windows with their lights out. I say no, and when he gets more insistent, when it starts to feel like pressure, I say, No, Michael, but after a while I start to wonder if he will keep calling if I don't let him come over, if I don't say yes, okay, come over.

. . .

Colleen makes me tell her about Dakeba and then she tells me that Michael is a player anyway. She says, It's good you have a boy somewhere else. What did you say his name was, Dakari? Michael talks to some girl up at his school, Washington, a cheerleader. You know he plays ball. I shake my head. Yeah, girl, he's a running back, or tight end, or something like that. "Little Red Corvette" comes on. Colleen says, Ooh, I love this song, and turns the volume knob on her stereo. Walking back to the bed from the record player, she stops in front of the mirror above her chest of drawers to put on some purplish lipstick, lipstick that looks good against her dark skin, lipstick that would look stupid on me. I watch her watching herself, the way she stands in front of the mirror looking straight at her own reflection, without making faces or squinting, the way I do.

I don't tell Colleen that Michael came to my house on one of those nights we were on the phone except my mother was away writing and I was alone. He told me he had a sore throat and I told him that I could make him some tea. I don't know where what I told him came from, but it came out, this voice that was mine saying all these grown, seductive things. He needed someone to take care of him, he needed someone to make him tea. I had my voice all lowered and the mouthpiece of the phone pressed against my lips. I said I would do all that for him. His voice got soft and he told me he'd be over in fifteen minutes.

He came. I put on my mother's leopard-print camisole and a big red robe we shared to hide it. I made him tea, honey, and lemon like my mother made me when I was sick. I sat him down on the velvet sofa from the secondhand store and then I lied. I told him I wasn't a virgin and I had done this lots of times. He told me it was okay to be a virgin, and I said, Yeah, but I'm not one. We went into my mother's study because I thought if he saw my room with Michael Jackson posters and rainbows everywhere, he would know I wasn't fifteen. We lay down on the mattress on the floor and then he climbed on top of me and pushed his penis inside of me.

Afterward, after it hurt and after I didn't know whether I had felt what I was supposed to feel, he got up, told me he had a curfew, and headed for the door. I walked behind him, stood there in the doorway as he kissed me, pushing me against the white wall there, and then I locked the door behind him.

Colleen is parting Asha's hair, making neat lines down the dome of little Asha's head. I watch her, transfixed by the way she dips her finger into the pot of yellow Afro-Sheen while she holds on to the hair she is about to braid, dabs the stuff onto Asha's scalp, and then, like some kind of lizard or snake, runs her fingers through the tuft of hair, leaving a smooth, perfectly formed plait in the aftermath. I want to tell Colleen what happened, but I think she might think I'm fast or a slut. I am not sure I can trust her to keep it between us. She is Michael's friend, after all, she has known him since they were kids. I am just the new girl, everyone is still checking me out.

L ena and I are fighting, kicking
and grunting and losing our bal-
ance. Falling across the back of the orange couch in her living
room. Lena is stronger than I am, stronger than I thought she
would be, and as she scratches the side of my face I think that for
a white girl, she can fight. She fights with fingernails and big pro-
peller arms that beat down on my back, making a hollow thumping sound when they hit. Lena has some experience fighting; she
fought the big Samoan girl up at school, Lynn. Lynn had slapped
her and then walked off, and she, Lena, had gone after her, grabbing the back pocket of Lynn's jeans to spin her around. The
pocket had ripped off in Lena's hand, and then they started swinging. It all started when Lynn called Lena a slut and Lena told Lynn
that at least that was better than being a dog.

We are on the floor, knees rubbing against the yellow-green
carpet, when Papa, Lena's father, comes home. We don't hear him
come in, but we hear when he says, What are my girls doing? That
stops us. He pulls us apart, disbelief on his face. He steers me
toward his study, the little room he writes in after teaching high

school history all day, the room that he sleeps in, too, when he and Lena's mom don't sleep together, which is often.

Papa is a thin man, and gentle, with a ruddy face and greenish eyes and white-gray hair that falls over his forehead. I can't remember when I start calling him Papa, what incident brought us that close, but I hug him a lot, reaching my arms around his bony frame and pressing my cheek against the slick cotton of his cool madras shirts. Papa fought in World War Two. His favorite movie is *Das Boot* and he watches it again and again from his easy chair in the living room, reliving, I guess, his days in the navy.

Lena's mother works at IBM and pretended not to be a Jew in Germany during the war. She is stern and hard, tall and blond, guilty about surviving and estranged from her mother, who lives in Switzerland. There is love between Lena's parents, but it is a dark, formal understanding rather than a giddy Hallmark kind of thing. It reeks of obligation, desperation, and other unspeakable truths. It doesn't occur to me until much later that the bond between Lena's parents might have something to do with the war, with Lena's father being in the liberating army and Lena's mother waiting to be liberated.

Papa sits me down in his study and puts Pink Floyd's *The Wall* on the phonograph. He plugs in the headphones and adjusts them over my ears until I hear the sounds of helicopters and marching feet. Then the guitar riff. Then *Daddy's flown across the ocean, leaving just a memory.* And then he leaves me to sit in the cave of a room that Lena and I sometimes hide out in late at night, listening to Zeppelin and the Police and Stevie Nicks long after we are supposed to be asleep.

Those nights, Lena and I pilfer weed from the bottom drawer

of Papa's desk, get fantastically stoned, and obsess over how to mask our red eyes and feed our hungry stomachs. Off balance and giggling, Lena digs around in her purse for the Visine. Squinting into the medicine cabinet mirror, we take turns jabbing the plastic tip into our eyeballs. Then we trip down the hall and into the kitchen to make tacos with Lowry's taco seasoning. I cut up tomatoes while Lena grates cheese and browns a big package of bloody ground beef, and then we sit around her Scandinavian wood table stuffing our faces, scooping up taco meat with our fingers and cracking up.

how memory works how memory how
y works how memory works how mem
rks how memory works how memor
ow memory works how memory work
mory works how memory works how
y works how memory works how mem
rks how memory works how memor
ow memory works how memory work
memory works how memory works how
works how memory works how mem
rks how memory works how memor
ow memory works how memory work
memory works how memory works how
rks how memory works how memor
ow memory works how memory work
mory works how memory works how
works how memory works how mem
ks how memory works how memor
orks how memory works how memor

I meet Lena one day out in the square. She is roller-skating and we say hello to each other and then a few days later there she is, gliding up the concrete walk on roller skates, stopping in front of my building. Lanky, pale, with stringy brown hair pulled back into a ponytail. She must have seen my mother out on the balcony watering because it is Mama who calls me outside. I look down, leaning out over the flower boxes, and it is Lena, asking if I want to hang out. I don't think, Oh, here is this white girl, even though it must register. What I like is her devil-may-care attitude, the way she squints up at me, sure I will come down.

It isn't long before I am a regular at her house and she at mine. When my mother is away working, we throw parties full of white boys with feathered hair and ripped-up jean jackets and thick white girls in tight skirts and tan leather boots that stick out from the bottoms of their leg warmers. In the living room and kitchen, kids smoke pot and drink from six-packs of Miller and Michelob and Budweiser. In the bathroom, kids pee and vomit. Lena lures in her boy of the moment and spends the evenings winding

around under him on the living room sofa, while I prowl from
room to room making sure things are under control, that nothing
is on fire, that no one is sneaking into my mother's bedroom to
have sex. Out of the corner of my eye, I watch Lena's tongue slip
in and around some boy's mouth, and chart her hands rubbing
the hardness bulging against her crotch.

Part of being like Lena, connected to Lena, I'm not sure which,
has to do with being open to crazy shit, to fixing my face to say that
I will try anything, sure. One night I take a Quaalude. Fucked up,
numb, only vaguely in touch with reality, I watch a pizza box catch
fire in the oven while one of the boys dangles a girl over the rail-
ing of the balcony. When I wake up the next morning I have bruises
all over my body I can't explain. The next weekend Lena and I
score some acid, and just as we start tripping, her father calls her
home. Scared out of my mind, I spend the night huddled in a blanket outside on the balcony, praying for the blinking lights in my
head to go out, for the sun to come up, for Lena to come back to me.

It also has to do with sex. I tell Lena about Michael and she
tells me about her boyfriends. We talk about how they kiss and
whether or not they have big dicks and how much we like them or
how much we like someone else and want to go out with him instead. One day after we've gone skating in Japantown, Lena and I
walk over to the Planned Parenthood on Post Street and fill out
forms while we wait to be seen by the doctor. We both want to be
on the pill, and after we talk to the doctors and get examined, we
walk out onto the street with little pink dispensers of pills called
Ortho-Novum. I'm not sure I really need the pill because I'm not
having sex regularly, just that one time with Michael, but since
Lena is getting them I figure I should too.

L ena is adopted, though I don't find that out until much later. In the beginning it all looks normal, nuclear. Lena's two married, working parents; Lena, the rebellious teen. I knock on her bedroom window from the outside and she comes bounding out into the hallway to let me in. If we are going skating she glides out in her skates, which make her even taller than she already is, Amazon tall. Her skates are the expensive professional kind, the white ones that look like ice skates but have wheels instead of blades. She rolls to the door, opens it with her key ring jangling full of dollar-ninety-nine items like a mini metal tee shirt that says *Born to Skate* and a tiny plastic photo holder with a picture of her golden retriever squeezed into it. I wait for her to open the door in my red and white skates and jade green velour sweatshirt Danita and I bought on sale at Macy's. My skates are clunky, cheap, and awkward next to Lena's graceful ones. We skate through our square and over to Geary, the big boulevard between our housing complex, the square, and Japantown.

Japantown is where I pretend to be Lena's skating coach. It

is where, in front of the peace pagoda on the slick gray slate tiles there, I count for her—one and two and three and four—before she does her axels, where I spot her, looking on with maternal concern as she clatters to the ground. Japantown is where Lena and I buy cigarettes from the vending machine by the Ginza, where we smoke the cigarettes, Benson & Hedges Lights or Newports or Marlboros, hiding behind a public stage used every year for the Cherry Blossom Festival. Sometimes we just go over there to smoke. Lena calls me up and says she is dying for a cigarette and I concur, and then we dodge all the traffic on Geary and run across to squat behind the stage, cupping our hands around the match flame to get our cigs going in the San Francisco wind.

Lena never asks me about race. She meets my mother and understands that I have a white father somewhere in New York, a white father she will never meet because why would she, my father never comes to San Francisco, and I can never imagine a time when Lena would be in New York, her earthy California-girl self adrift in a sea of taxis and skyscrapers. The closest we come to talking about color is one evening when Lena is getting dressed to go on a date with her boyfriend, Dave, the surfer who bought her a Boogie board and whom she meets early Saturday mornings down at Ocean Beach to get her surf on. She is putting on blush and telling me about him, about how they had had sex on the beach the night before and how good it was. Lena is laughing and cocking her narrow hips to one side of the sink. I ask her if he is cute and she begins to describe him. Oh yeah, she says, smiling into her own eyes in the mirror. He's got the best smile and the strongest, sexiest arms and legs. His skin is dark chocolate brown and he's got a cute little baby afro.

I meet Dave later, years later, and we have our own date at Ocean Beach, but instead of surfing we eat hot dogs at the Cliff House, the big seafood restaurant perched over the water, and then go into the arcade underneath. We take a strip of Polaroids, four black-and-white squares on top of one another that Michael finds tucked into my journal and goes ballistic over. In the bottom two Dave is kissing the side of my face, his big black hand pressing against the length of my pale gray neck.

By that time he has stopped seeing Lena, and I, for the most part, have too. Lena and I go to the same school, but I have been claimed by black girls and meaty football-playing boys while Lena stays true to her feathered, beer-drinking white friends. At lunchtime she sits on benches on one side of the football field while I sit on identical benches on the other side. We might say hello when we pass each other in the hallways, but mainly we pretend that we haven't grown up together, haven't been best friends, haven't spent countless nights and days together, sharing everything.

But of course it is even more complicated than that. Lena and I were as close as two girls could be, and then things get in between us, things like language and fashion and color. I feel every inch of our separation, miss her every time I choose to go with my black friends instead of with her. I wonder what she is doing when I wake up alone in my house on Saturday mornings, wanting to call her, wanting to be close the way we had been but not knowing how to cross that divide that is drawn somewhere I can't quite locate and by someone who doesn't seem to be me. It is more than growing apart, what happens between me and Lena, it is not knowing how to grow together, not knowing how to bring her into the world that is slowly claiming me, marking me, not knowing how to teach her how to walk and talk so that she can fit into my world, not knowing how to let her be her and fit in without doing any goddamn thing.

On the days we don't go skating, Lena holds the door open for me, leaning out without going down the step, keeping her balance there while I walk through and into the hallway and into her house that is so different from mine, so full of stuff where mine is spare and minimal. Plants hanging in macramé holders, chairs with hand-crocheted doilies draped over their backs, books about boats and World War Two and Jung, miniature ceramic animals, there is stuff everywhere. And in the back, there is a terrarium because Lena is always rescuing or caring for some creature. In the time I know her she has lizards, turtles, cats, dogs, rabbits, a ferret. She volunteers at the Junior Museum, cleaning out cages, learning about animals, bringing home whatever she finds roaming the streets.

When I walk in most times her parents aren't home, or if they are, I am such a regular they barely look up. Hi, Rebecca, you hungry? But Lena and I are already in her room, the first one up front, with the mirrored closet doors and the Stevie Nicks posters, the wetsuit in a heap by the unmade bed.

Or we are in the bathroom, getting ready to go: to the park, to Japantown, to school. I sit on the toilet seat under the bright lights while she twists the curling iron through her hair. I have a picture of myself somewhere taken in that bathroom, Lena's bathroom. I'm wearing a bright red jacket and flowery shirt. My hair is a curly mass, my lips are shining, my cheeks flushed.

I can't count on my hands and feet how many times I watch Lena get ready to go to Lone Pine, a wilderness up north where a friend of her father's photographs her a couple of weekends a month. It always seems glamorous to me, that Lena is going to be photographed by a man in the woods, though I always wonder why I can't go, why she doesn't invite me, who is so much of the time constantly at her side. That is strange to me, and also why she makes such a big deal out of how she looks before she goes, putting on mascara, eyeliner, blush, and crimping her hair, telling me the whole while that Pete likes her like this or like that, all the while getting ready by making herself look older, sexier, more masked. She doesn't tell me until high school, long after we have stopped talking every day, that Pete molested her for all those years, that she posed for him nude, and that she wants to press charges but is afraid to do it by herself.

It isn't until high school, at least five years after the whole thing had started, that we drive down to Half Moon Bay late one night when Lena says she can't sleep, to press charges against Pete with the local police. After the long drive, we unfold ourselves from the car and walk, shell shocked but determined, into the tiny police station at the end of a dark road, past a few of the big pumpkin patches Half Moon Bay is famous for. It is just us, two high school girls, one brown, one white, in jeans and tee shirts.

The police woman at the desk asks what we want, and when Lena doesn't say anything for a few seconds, I say, My friend here wants to file a report, she's been sexually assaulted. And then they take Lena into a room by herself and I sit down on a hard green bench and wait for her to come back.

On the way home Lena cries in the passenger seat of my mother's car while I adjust the controls to make sure she is warm enough, comfortable. I keep telling her that she has done the right thing, that he isn't going to hurt her, even though that is what she fears most. She imagines that he will come after her, saying it was her fault, she had asked for it, had been willing, which she was, more or less. The more was that when what they did didn't make her feel sick and ashamed, it made her feel special and attractive and powerful. The less was that she was thirteen and fourteen and twelve years old, he was a friend of her father's, and some part of her thought it was what she was supposed to do, some kind of rent she had to pay for being pretty. I keep telling her that there is no excuse.

That night Lena spends the night at my house, sleeping in my mother's big empty bed. We stay up late talking, about what happened between us, how we had been attracted to each other and not known what to do, how we had drifted apart and not known how to stop it, and about how Lena was adopted and determined to find her real parents. It is the first I hear of it, Lena's being adopted, and I am shocked to think of her belonging to some other people out in the world, some people we can't yet see, another set of parents. It makes a part of her unknown to me, the way I imagine a part of me, the part that left on holidays and after two years to go to New York, must have been impossible for her to see, an invisible face always lurking behind the one in front of her.

I don't remember what starts our fight. She has taken something of mine or gone somewhere without telling me. Whatever the particulars, they have nothing to do with what is really going on, that having more to do with desire and control and fear than any other mundane thing like a certain pair of pants or a date. We fight because we are so close we can't breathe, because there is no other way to release all the pent-up emotions that course between us. We want to touch, obviously, we want some physical acting out of the powerful feelings the other can arouse in us, and so we kick and scratch and bite. Before Papa comes in and separates us, I have a mouthful of Lena's light brown hair between my lips, can feel the strands coarse against my tongue. I feel relief there on the couch with my fingernails gouging into her skin. I can smell her, the milky blend of Silkience shampoo and patchouli oil, taste her. She is finally close enough.

STOP

M y mother takes my hand and leads me into her study. It's
the small room at the front of the apartment, the room to the left
when you first walk in the door. We walk past the single bed on
the floor, over to the window with the sliding glass pane, and stop
in front of her desk, an old wooden door on top of two file cabinets. From the corner of my eye I can see the fir tree outside, the
sky darkening, the fog rolling in. It is early evening. I have just re-
turned from Lucky's, the supermarket down the block and across
the street from the Ellis Street projects, where Mama sent me to
buy eggs and orange juice.

Standing there, one hip cocked against her chair, my mother
takes a small, wood-framed photograph down from the wall above
her old Smith-Corona and hands it to me. When Mama gives me
the photo to look at I am standing very close to her, our hips and
sides touching. As I look at the photograph, hold it in my hands,
she is quiet, waiting for me to respond. As I look, she slides her
arm underneath mine and lets it rest at my waist so that we are

linked like a chain, our flesh hooked at various places, our bodies connected.

The picture is of an older brown-skinned woman with a frowning face, partly bent over, leaning on a walking stick. She stands in a harsh and faded yellow light I associate with old cameras and dead people I will never meet. She wears a long dress and a weary pose. There are bundles, pale sacks full of objects I cannot determine, strapped to her back. She is outside, on a dirt road, in front of what look like felled trees but which are so tiny and hard to see they could be anything: the remains of a shack, a stack of lumber, wreckage from a storm. The image is so faded, I have to squint my eyes and bring the photograph to my nose to make out the woman's face, and still I cannot see her clearly.

As I look I have the uncanny feeling that I am supposed to know who this woman is, to recognize her face, her hands, her stance. But I don't. "This is your great-great-great-great-great-great-grandmother, May Poole," my mother says with great solemnity. "She was a slave." I scrutinize the blur that is Ms. Poole's face for some trace of my grandpa Willie Lee's half–Native American mother, or my grandma Minnie Lu's six-foot-tall sisters, the huge, solid women named Mildred and Malsenior that I have met only once or twice in my life. I look for the thread that makes the life of this ancestor intersect with my own. I feel lost.

And yet over the next several months I walk into my mother's study to see Grandmother Poole, to look into her face again, to read what my mother has typed and pasted beneath the fraying square: Ms. May Poole walked from Virginia to Florida with two babies on her hips, she was a slave. Slowly, and not all at once, I add my own thoughts: that I would not have been born had

Grandmother Poole not done her walking, had she not fought off whatever demons wanted to keep her from moving, from being free. I imagine how heavy the babies must have been, bundled to her breast and growing by the hour. I wonder how often she may have wanted to put them down and leave them, lying screaming beside the road, or fast asleep in the crook of a tree. I wonder if I would have been as brave.

I do not then, but later on I put her image in my mind alongside my great-grandma Jennie: they are, together, my oldest known ancestors. But when I see them in my mind's eye, grayhaired Grandma Jennie staring squarely into the lens and Grandmother Poole looking out, exhausted, over the hill, I cannot help but wonder if either of them ever could have fully claimed and embraced me. If as an anonymous child I walked up to Grandmother Poole unannounced she might have cared for me, might have extended herself for my well-being, but wouldn't she also see the lightness of my skin as a sign of danger, the evidence of brutality? Wouldn't part of her heart necessarily then, out of self-preservation, close to me? And if I were to happen upon my great-grandma Jennie, my hair bushy and my skin brown, wouldn't she ignore me, or shoo me away like a bothersome fly, like a little nigger child in her way, a child of one of the tenants in the Harlem apartments she owned with her husband, a child whose parents owe rent?

L isa Green in Mrs. Thompson's
math class, six seats behind me,
staring bored out the window. Lisa Green walking in the school-
yard, she on one side of the squares of the metal fence, glaring at
me on the other. Lisa Green strutting down the hallway, a chain
with her keys on one end dangling from low-slung perfectly
creased burgundy chinos. Lisa Green on the bus, the 44, sitting in
the back, knee up, foot resting on the hump above the wheel, the
only thing girl about her the two lemon yellow barrettes closed
around her thick, mixed-race hair. But then on other days she's all
curves: full breasts buttoned into a Mandarin-style top, hair up in
a bun, tight black skirt, pointy red shoes bought or maybe stolen
from Emporium Capwell, the big department store on Market
Street. Lisa as cocktail waitress at Szechwan Delight. Lisa as pros-
titute from a movie on Vietnam.

L isa and me lying in the back room of her house at three A.M.,
in our underwear. We're lying head to foot, smoking New-

ports and blowing smoke rings. There's a little portable radio next to us on the bare, dirty, blue-striped mattress playing "Happy Anniversary." A brother singing *And I remember, I remember when we used to play shoot 'em up.* It's KSOL's late-night show, and whenever we're at Lisa's house we listen to it, to the DJ with the low, smooth voice playing old love songs from back in the day, songs that Danita remembers when they come on the radio while we're in her car, the burgundy Cutlass Supreme, songs that make her shake her head and say, Damn, I remember when this came out, I was in high school, dating such and such a boy.

It's dusty and dirty back here in this room, because Lisa's mother never comes back here, and the only time it gets any use is when Lisa or her sister brings friends to do stuff they can't do out in the open, like smoke herb and drink wine coolers out of brown paper bags. Back here there isn't even a TV, like the one that's always on in the front room, where Lisa's tiny light-skinned mother sits watching her stories: *As the World Turns, One Life to Live,* and *All My Children*; and where we sit, me, Lisa, her mother, and her sister, Lori, some Saturday mornings watching *Soul Train* with Don Cornelius and *American Bandstand* with Dick Clark. Back here there is only the radio playing love songs and a blue bulb Lisa stole from Lucky's screwed into an old lamp base.

When we're back here, Lisa and I talk about people. The skinny black girl with the nasty scar down her face. That red-headed boy who comes to school late, not like twenty minutes late but like after-lunch late. The cute Mexican boy with the shiny black hair, Chris, who has a crush on me. Susan, Lisa's best friend who used to threaten to beat me up, way back before Lisa and me became friends and Lisa put a stop to all that. We don't talk about

Lisa and her mother and sister being poor. We don't talk about how they all three sleep on one lumpy mattress, how when Lisa's mother sends us to the store for eggs and milk, she gives us food stamps, how the only heat in the house comes from the oven.

No. I tell her about Michael and what cologne he wears, One Man Show, and all the gory details of what we do when we fool around. She asks me if I like to suck it. I don't know what she means at first, but then I'm lying to keep up. Yeah, yeah, I like to suck it, I say. But it's too big. Lisa cracks up. Too big? Girl, don't you know it ain't ever too big?

Lisa is short, much shorter than me but in her family she is the tallest and the darkest. Her mother and sister are near white and tiny, maybe four feet eleven. Her mother's head reaches maybe to my breast bone, and with Lori it's the same way. Even though it's clear that they do, I don't think to myself that Lisa and Lori must have different fathers, I guess because we don't ever talk about fathers, neither of us has one that's anywhere around at the moment and in her house the whole idea seems like a moot point. Lisa's is a family of women. No man ever comes home, and the only time men are mentioned is when Lisa's mother says something in Spanish about all the boys calling Lisa on the phone and how Lisa better be careful with all those boys. She don't want no *bebé*.

Lisa has lots of boys after her because she's cute and fast. She has a big butt and big breasts and a pretty smile. She's in the sixth grade like me, but a year older because she got left back. All of her boyfriends are way older, they're in high school or working already: construction, food service, UPS. Tonight Lisa's talking about Joe, Marvin's brother, and how she's through with him. I met Joe one night when we walked over to his building in the middle of the night. Lisa told him we were looking for weed when really we were looking for him. It was Lisa's big idea to go after the Creature Feature movie went off Channel Eleven and the screen went blank but we were still wide awake. I put on a striped hooded sweatshirt I got from the five-dollar bin at the Esprit outlet, and my jelly shoes.

Joe was on the other end of a few dark, deserted streets, watching *Friday Nite Videos* with Marvin. The two of them were like angel and devil. Joe had a big round face, big perfect teeth, and an easy laugh. Marvin was pointy, all chin, nose, and ears, with eyes that darted around a lot, like he was waiting for someone to sneak up on him. We smoked some weed and Joe gave Lisa a little Baggie full to take back to my house, even though we didn't leave for hours. Even though they disappeared into the bedroom and left me alone in the living room with Marvin until five in the morning.

Lisa says she's leaving Joe 'cause he's stingy, he doesn't give her enough. I nod and say, Yeah, you betta cut him loose. But I'm not really sure what Joe's not giving her. Money? Sex? Attention? Weed? Lisa doesn't need any more clothes, she's got a whole closet full of red and fuchsia and yellow outfits from Emporium and Penney's and Millers Outpost and Mervyn's, stuff she steals on weekend trips to Serramonte. Lisa's really good at stealing. She walks around the store picking skirts and blouses off the racks, holding things up to her body in front of mirrors like she's gonna buy them. The security guards don't pay her any mind because she calls attention to herself, asking me all loud in front of them if I think whatever she's looking at is cute, or will it match the striped jacket she has at home. When they turn around she stuffs it into her bag or up under her shirt, then tells me to come on and follow her out the door.

I stole with Lisa at Mervyn's one time. I took this see-through jelly jacket I didn't really want. I didn't have enough to buy it and Lisa told me it would be easy to steal 'cause it was a jacket and I wasn't wearing one and so if I just put it on over my clothes it would look like I had walked in with it. We went out to Serramonte on one of those Caltrans buses, like the one I took with Bethany to see her mother the year before, and Susan came with us. It was toward the beginning of the year and so I didn't know either of them too well, only that Susan had called me a yellow bitch and told me I thought I was better than everybody else, and Lisa had been her backup, trailing behind her and saying they should both, together, kick my ass. I don't remember how it all got turned around, how come Lisa left Susan and came for me, but I'm sure stealing that jelly jacket at Mervyn's and joining those I couldn't beat, attaching myself to people who hated me as an act of self-protection, had something to do with it.

We went into the store like we always did, casually, like we had pockets full of money, which we didn't. I might have had the twenty dollars my mother left me on the table when she went away for the week, or less if I had paid my bus fare or eaten lunch and dinner a couple of times. Lisa had even less, a few dollar bills and maybe a five for emergencies secreted away in the tiny square pocket in the front of her jeans. Susan, with her dirty jeans, scarred face, and natty, partially pressed hair, had even less than that, maybe a roll of quarters balled up in her fist. When we came out, Lisa had a new shirt, I had the jacket, and Susan had a bottle of bright pink Revlon fingernail polish. We ran shrieking and doubled over through the parking lot, toward the bus stop, giddy and high on our badness. But when we finally climbed on the bus and sat down, it got real quiet. Lisa stared out the window, Susan stared at me, I stared at all the other riders. A dead end. No one had stopped us, caught us, nothing. No one cared.

After "Happy Anniversary" goes off and then "When We Get Married" does too, Lisa asks me if I see myself getting married and to who and how do I wanna live. For a second I'm surprised, taken aback. I haven't been in my own mind, thinking thoughts about boyfriends or what I want to be when I grow up, I've been watching Lisa's full lips blow smoke rings, the way she holds the cigarette, not between her fore and middle fingers like girls are supposed to but between her forefinger and her thumb like a guy. I've been watching her eyes move beneath the lids, noticing how naked they seem without the heavy black eyeliner she usually wears.

Luckily Lisa breaks in before I can answer. She says she wants a big house and cars and a man who has Bank. When she says Bank she slaps one hand, top down, onto the mattress for emphasis. He gotta have Bank. It's cold and so I push my legs a little closer to Lisa's torso, feeling for the warmth there. I think of *Dynasty,* the show we watch on Wednesday nights with Krystal, Alexis, Blake, and Bobby Jo. I think of the opening credits, when they're flying over the big houses and swimming pools, the circular driveways full of fancy cars, and then the writing in cursive like on the cover of the Harlequin romance novels Lisa reads: *Dynasty.*

I can't imagine being married and I tell her so. My mama's not married and she says it's better that way. To have people come to visit you when you want to see them, but that to live together all the time is crazy, unhealthy. I guess that sounds right to me and I tell Lisa that. It would be okay if I was alone, with my man coming to see me when I wanted him to, I say, not married. As for Bank, well, I don't know. Lisa says, Girl, you crazy, and I shrug, pull back a little, and take a drag of my Newport. The menthol in the smoke hits my lungs like a little stab but I don't put it out.

The truth is I don't really think that far ahead. Lying next to Lisa on the dirty mattress in the cold room is enough for me. It fills all of my senses and I don't think about hardly anything else. Maybe somewhere in the back of my mind I'm thinking about what my mother would say if she saw me. I'm wondering if she could imagine what Lisa's house is like, and what we do back here in this little room. It's not like a whole conscious thought or anything, but somewhere I feel like maybe I want my mother to find out that where I am may not be very safe and I want her to tell me to come home. I want her to tell me that I can't go so far away from her while I'm so young, I can't get on the 44 late at night and ride to the other side of San Francisco to spend the night with people she doesn't know, with people she's never seen.

But that's just a feeling I have, some picture in my mind that has no words that's buried underneath everything else. Under Newports and being like Lisa. I don't want to think about that so I just let my eyes close when they want to, lift the cig to my mouth every few minutes, and let my body vibrate from the sounds on the radio. Even though I have different feelings underneath, it still mostly feels like I love it back here, the way it feels like we're in our own spaceship, gliding through a quiet, sleepy universe; the way I feel so close to Lisa and not alone, the way her toughness, how she always seems to know what she wants, makes it easier for me to lope along at her side, pretending to move in ways that come natural to her, to Lisa Green, a half-Spanish girl living with her mother and sister in a tiny rundown house in Hunter's Point, but not to me.

L isa and me up at Wilson, one of the toughest high schools in the city. There's no way we'd be up here if Lisa's sister didn't go here, if Lisa couldn't say she was Pookie's sister and get people's respect. People being the hard-looking black, white, and Latino kids hanging out on the wall outside the school in Members Only jackets and their boyfriends' football jerseys. When we get there, I walk next to Lisa, switching my hips, squaring my shoulders, tilting my head to one side and pretending I don't see the kids on the wall. It's the same walk I put on when we go to the projects in the middle of the night, or when we get on the bus and walk to the back where all the boys are sitting smoking weed. From Lisa I learn to move like I know where I'm going, like I could be dangerous if talked to the wrong way, like I have brothers or uncles who would come out of nowhere to protect me if something should go down.

It's the end of the school year and the seniors are putting on a strut show. I've never been to a strut show and so Lisa, Miss Experience, pulls me along, making the plans. "Wear those tight jeans and that yellow shirt." "Darnell said he would pick us up from my house and take us over there, but we have to take the bus back, so bring enough money." "Girl, I'm a wear my black pants with the red stripe up the leg and that red shirt with the fringes. I think Joe might come. It's gonna be live." Lisa's talking fast, mapping the scene out for me as I lie back on the brass bed my mom bought for me at Cost Plus, and wrap the curly red cord of my Trimline around my legs. I hold up my end of the conversation, popping my gum and shooting the shit back, but there's something that's not quite right. There's a part of me that worries about being out of my element, out of control, with only Lisa as my guide.

The show is good, like nothing I've ever seen before. Black boys with big afros and shags in silver from head to toe, silver suits, silver spray-painted faces and arms and hair, coming out of a big silver spaceship. They're dancing to Stetsasonic and Parliament, and when they move onstage, under the red and orange and blue strobe lights of the school auditorium, they look half human and half robot, five or six boys jerking their arms and legs in sync with one another and the music. Even before they get halfway into their routine, we all are up in the audience, yelling and screaming and waving the smoke from the smoke machine out of our faces, swaying our hands and hips and doing The Rock in the aisles.

Afterward, we all rush out into the streets in one big mass. Black, brown, yellow, and white arms and legs and sneakered feet, pouring down the hill from the school to the bus stop. There are girlfriends hooked into the crooks of their boyfriends' elbows, groups of girls in matching cheerleader jackets showing off new steps under pools of light streaming from lampposts, wild boys with picks tucked into the backs of their afros wearing Adidas shell-toes and burgundy Lees walking down the middle of the street, daring the cars, puffing on Newports.

Lisa is carried away by the flow of the crowd and so am I, but while she's inside of it, calling to friends of her sister's I don't know, flirting with boys who pull at her long braids, I'm removed, anonymous, new, caught up in the excitement but also flying overhead, studying the scene, looking for my insertion point. Where do I put myself? At the bottom of the hill, the crowd rounds the corner like a big slow animal, and then whoosh, quick as lightning, there's a mood change and folks start running. At first I think they're trying to catch the bus I see up ahead, a 15 that has its lights on, paused at the stop sign and waiting patiently for its fares, but then I notice a crowd circling what looks like two high school girls, and I know there's trouble. Lisa grabs the cuff of my shirt and drags me toward the bus. And then we're in the thick of it, and suddenly it's like all the cold air has been sucked away and there's just the heat of bodies pressed against each other, the smell of curl activator, Ponds lotion, and Shalimar perfume, and this angry, busting-out kind of energy that has folks elbowing their way up to the front.

Up front is where the fight is. Two girls shouting over some dude named Lawrence who is nowhere in sight. One girl is dipping her fingers into a jar of Vaseline and slathering the gooey thickness all over her cinnamon-brown skin. The other girl is taking her earrings off, rolling up her sleeves. She looks scared, this one rolling up her sleeves, and I notice that unlike the girl with the Vaseline, she doesn't have friends behind her holding her jacket and telling her they have her back.

Some boys who know the story rush the two of them and egg them on. C'mon, Monica, you better beat her ass. You better get to stompin' this bitch. After what she did to you. And then it's on. The crowd starts saying yeah uh huh and what's taking you so long, you dirty ho. They're talking to the girl who's scared, the one looking around wildly, the one who looks like she's gonna lose 'cause she doesn't have the mind game. They've already decided that they're not on her side. They don't want the underdog, they want the winner. And then it starts. Monica the Vaseline girl swings and grabs at the other girl's hair, and then the other girl rams her head into Monica's stomach and then Monica starts punching her face with a balled-up fist.

When the girl starts bleeding, from her nose, her mouth, her ear, I can't tell which, the crowd roars. Some of the boys use the tips of their fingers to pull themselves up the side of the parked bus. Within seconds, there are twenty of them standing on top of it, slapping five and talking about having ringside seats. The bus driver, the adult, does nothing. He waits it out a few steps from his bus, beside some bushes, smoking a cigarette. When I look over at Lisa I see that she's grinning, shaking her head, even though I've got this queasy feeling rising up from the pit of my stomach. I am the girl "getting beat." If I shut my eyes I could be her, scared, sweaty, scratched, alone.

L isa and me. It's the end of sixth grade, summertime and I'm packing to go back east for the summer and the next two years. Lisa and I haven't talked, really, about what my leaving means for our friendship, though she does say she'll write me when I'm in New York and she's sure I'm going to forget about her when I'm gone. When she says this I just shrug my shoulders. I'm leaving so much: my mother, my friends, my Trimline phone, my bookshelves that were built just for me, Double Rainbow ice cream, and Michael. Roller-skating with Lena in Golden Gate Park, the square, Papa, Ocean Beach. The bus system I'm just beginning to know like the back of my hand. My savings account at Hibernia Bank.

I'm leaving so much and I have no idea what I'm getting in return, only that moving is already the thing I'm used to, changing my face and tongue already feels like some alchemical reaction that happens when the seasons change, when it's time for me to start a new school, or pack for summer, or pack to go to the other parent's house. It's a process of forgetting that happens, an erasure that starts gradually, as things are winding down, and picks up speed so that by the time I'm on the plane or bus I've forgotten almost all of what I've come from. I'm only in the present, driving up to the airport, waiting still on the escalator as it carries me closer to the gate. I'm an amnesiac because if I weren't I'd be feeling all that loss, all that tearing away, and who wants to feel that?

L isa. I'm upstairs, in my room, inching the door to the fire escape open so I can peek out and see who is ringing the bell without them seeing me. It's Lisa. I can see the top of her round head, the red sweatshirt she wears with the plaid pockets sewed onto the front. She's ringing the bell hard and long, like she's afraid someone might miss her if she announced herself any quieter. She's been ringing for a little while and she's starting to look impatient. Every minute or so she backs up and looks up at my window, peering with her tiny black eyes into my closed shutters. I can tell by the questioning look on her face that she's trying to figure out if it would be all right to call up to me, to shout my name loud enough for me to hear it three flights up.

I close the door and sit cross-legged in front of the full-length mirror my mother and I bought to share at Cost Plus. It's a fake brass number, with handles on either side for tilting it frontward and back, and I've parked it in front of my wall heater, across from my desk. Pushing my nose up close to the cool hard surface, I study my face: my brown eyes and pinkish-brown lips, my curly frizzy hair, the freckles across the bridge of my nose, the beauty marks thrown onto my left cheek. As Lisa rings and rings, my breath fogs up the glass and then inhales it clear again. I don't get up.

Lisa comes to my house two more times. Both times I peek out the door and then ignore her, watching with curious satisfaction as she mashes the buzzer again and again before stomping her foot or cursing into the air. The last time she comes, she looks up into the window and directly at me. My stomach is churning and I break into a sweat, but I do not answer the door. I never see Lisa again.

I don't have a daily routine, some set of rituals I perform without fail that give shape and body to my days and, by extension, my life. I don't wake up to an alarm, make coffee or squeeze juice, read the paper, watch the Weather Channel, climb into my car, and go to work. There's no unchanging workplace, the desk with the phone, the coworkers going in and out of the mailroom, polite conversations breaking up the monotony, concentration broken by glances at the clock. When the clock strikes or the sun goes down, I don't get back in my car or onto the subway. I don't arrive home, leaf through my mail, start supper, watch a little telly, and make a few calls. I don't climb into my bed, thumb some magazines, and drift off to my slumber, only to get up in eight to ten and start the whole thing again. I don't relax into a routine, I don't embrace a schedule. That is not my life.

Yet I long for such a routine, though more artisan than nine to five. I fantasize that a daily pattern that rarely changes would be soothing, and yet when I try to set one for myself, to do certain things at certain times, over a prolonged period, a month, say, there's something snaky and subterranean that rises to undermine my plan, pulling me from the desk, the pool, the routine. Settling in, moving from time slot to time slot, activity to activity feels, too calm, studied. It looks too much like the normal life I always wanted but never had. After a few days anxiety kicks in and I feel like a sitting duck waiting to be blown to bits, waiting for the winds of change to blow my calm asunder.

I am not rooted in the everyday. I move from place to place like a sybarite in search of pleasure, always thinking the final resting place will be just around the corner, at the end of this plane ride, behind the next door. I can never release myself from the mercurial aspects, can't allow myself to stand on some kind of ground. Instead I tend toward that which destabilizes and feels most like home: change, impermanence, a cursed quality pattern of in and out, here and there, city to city, place to place.

Houses are temporary containers. Some walls, a roof, a bathroom. I have exchanged spaces more times than I can count. I transition easily from neighborhood to neighborhood, coast to coast. I unpack and pack my belongings, shedding some and picking up others with ease and economy. The Miles Davis disc stays, Squeeze goes. The Esprit pants go, the Levi's stay. *The Diary of Anne Frank* stays, the Derrida reader goes. Letting go and holding on, letting go and holding on, this is the only constant. Not the people I love, not the person I become in their arms, under their gaze. There is only this process I have that is familiar: putting the sofa there, the books in stacks against that wall, hammering the nail for the painting here.

I don't trust the everyday; it is a mask, a sham. It gives the illusion of permanence, of an unshatterable calm, a placid surface; and yet underneath the pot is slowly coming to a boil. Each configuration is already breeding its own dialectical response, its own disintegration. I want to be prepared.

is my favorite part of Color War Sing is my favorite part of Color War Sing is my favorite part of Color War Sing is my favorite part of Color War Sing is my favorite part of Color War Sing is my favorite part of Color War Sing is my favorite part of Color War Sing is my favorite part of Color War Sing is my favorite part of Color War Sing is my favorite part of Color War Sing is my favorite part of Color War Sing is my favorite part of Color War Sing is my favorite part of Color War Sing is my favorite part of Color War Sing is my favorite part of Color War Sing is my favorite part of Color War Sing is my favorite part of Color War Sing is my favorite part of Color War Sing is my favorite part of Color War Sing is my favorite part of Color War Sing

PHOENICIA

Jay Schwartz is playing Pac-Man,
and Laurel Paci and I are standing
a little to his right, watching him eat the dots. Everyone knows
that Jay has a book that has patterns of the boards, patterns that
show you how to eat the most dots without getting caught, including how to get the floating bonus fruits: the cherry, the banana, the apple. When Jay is playing, a bunch of us crowd around
the game trying to memorize the way he moves the joystick and
pushes his guy through the mazes without getting eaten. Jay's twin
brother, Neil, plays the same way only not as well. The high scores
that come up at the end of each game go Jay (JAS) Jay (JAS) Jay
(JAS) Neil (NAS) Jay (JAS) Neil (NAS) Neil (NAS) Neil (NAS).

Instead of watching Jay's Pac-Man, I watch him, sneaking
looks when he is concentrating on the hardest boards, the ones
that take all his concentration even though he knows the patterns
by heart. The Schwartzes are the most popular boys at camp. They
have hazel eyes, perfect skin, and what look like ten-thousand-
dollar smiles. Their father is a television producer, which makes
them cooler than everybody else, and they live in Scarsdale, which

makes them richer. They wear their purple Scarsdale High varsity jackets to socials and at night to the canteen. I know them because on the first day of camp we take the same bus up to Phoenicia, the bus that leaves from the White Plains Mall, from in front of Caldor's, where we always shop at the last minute for stuff I need: a flashlight and batteries, a canteen, a plastic rain poncho.

It doesn't matter how unpopular or popular you are in school, at camp it's different, a whole new fishbowl. And so if you share the bus with someone coming up to camp, that means you see their mother and father and what kind of car they drive and who is there saying goodbye and if and how long they hold on to their parents or if they cry. You know they have a past and they know you do too and that makes you more naked to the people you ride the bus with, you can't pretend in front of them. The Schwartzes know that I know where they come from, and so we have that and that is why we always say hello to each other. That is our connection: the bus.

I am constantly aware of them, constantly looking at them because wherever they go they are the center of attention, setting an unspoken standard. When Jay picks up his girlfriend Wendy and swings her around in front of the mess hall, I watch her enviously: thin, with perfect white teeth, wavy light brown hair, a worn-out college football jersey that says *Schwartz* on the back thrown over her official green Fire Lake counselor's tee shirt. When one of the brothers strolls up the hill from the lake where we go swimming and boating, I watch them, the way they joke with girls from upper camp that they know, girls from the Lodge or the Ranch who flirt with them shamelessly, girls with gold Hebrew letter *chai*s around their necks, or Jewish stars. Girls with names like Andi Hirsch, Nanci Katz, Jodi Berman, Rachel Shapiro, Leslie Rosen, and Rebecca Leventhal.

I am one of three black girls at camp. There are no black boys. There is me, and this big tall strong girl named Rachel West and her little sister Michelle who live in New Rochelle. Rachel and I don't talk much. It is like if we talk to each other everyone around might notice that we are black, and neither of us wants that. Rachel is an athlete, she is always picked first for Color War teams, and has a full mouth of braces that make her lips stick out. Her hair is long and half-straightened and you can see the big bush of it from far away, even when it is all pulled back with a ponytail holder.

There are maybe three hundred and fifty kids at camp, all of us ruled by college-age counselors: two per bunk, and two head counselors, Alice for Girls Camp and Sy for Boys. Alice is in her forties and has a curly perm which frizzes in the heat. She wears jeans that are too tight even on the hottest days, and never smiles. She smokes long thin cigarettes, and when she comes over to our activity during the day to talk to a counselor, everybody gets kind of quiet and on best behavior.

Sy is totally crazy and looks like a shorter, dumpier Albert Einstein. Some mornings he wakes up the camp playing a bugle out of tune over the all-camp PA, or he sings, off-key, old songs I have never heard before. He plays a lot of tennis, and when he walks by an activity swinging an old beat-up racket, it is like God passing, this crazy force who controls everything, this funky weird old man who mutters to himself while he walks down the road between the mail shack, where we pick up care packages filled with candy and

Pop-Tarts and Cheez Whiz and marshmallows that our grandmothers send, and the rec hall, where we put on productions of *Bye Bye Birdie* and *Fiddler on the Roof.*

It is Sy's camp, those of us interested in things like ownership come to understand this. Alice has to get permission for everything from him, which is why she is always on his porch with her clipboard and pencil in hand, and he is the one who masterminds all the Color War fake-outs and breakouts. One year the whole camp was watching *Fiddler on the Roof* in the rec hall after we had been screaming One Two Three Four We Want Color War, Five Six Seven Eight We Don't Want to Wait and banging our cups and plates on the table in the mess hall. When Tevya was singing his song on the roof and he is supposed to say Tradition, Tradition, he said Color War, Color War instead and we all were stunned for a second and then all of these pieces of paper, some green and some white, fluttered down from the rafters that announced two teams, the White Buccaneers and the Green Pirates, and there were lists too, and every bunk was split in half into Green and White and each team had to report to a different set of bleachers.

But after we all split up and got bummed out that we weren't on the same team as our friends, then our counselors told us that it wasn't a real breakout but a fake-out, and then we all went back to our bunks wondering when the real thing was going to happen and when we were going to see the whole *Fiddler on the Roof* show. Breakout came when the whole camp was assembled for a visit from former president Ford. An impersonator drove up in an open-top limousine, and just as he stepped out and approached the podium, a helicopter filled with Secret Service dropped the green and white lists, and then we really did split up and then

Color War, with all of its tallying up of points at the end of long days of basketball, swimming, and kayak races, and all of its frantic alma mater learning in preparation for the final, ultimate competition, Sing Night, began for real.

Sing is my favorite part of Color War. I love the corny romantic songs about Fire Lake, I love standing up on the benches, pounding my fist in the air to encourage the younger campers to keep up, to punch up the emotion. Sing is the heart of Color War, the heart and the drama. Even if your team is down by more than a hundred points, you can still pull an upset on Sing Night if your songs are good and if your team sings them with enough feeling. And since it is your big shot, everybody sings like they won't ever need their vocal chords again, especially the little kids from lower camp who sit in the front row and don't really have a clue how important it all is. On Sing Night though they miraculously figure it out and stand there in front of their benches, mesmerized by the fist of whoever is leading the Sing, whoever is standing on that bench in front of us all, pounding the air.

And then after Sing it is all over, one team or the other wins and you can finally be friends again with your bunkmates on the other team, the ones you haven't spoken to in eight days. And then everybody puts their arms around everybody else and walks back from the rec hall, exhausted, burned out from all-night Sing rehearsals, all-night mural painting sessions, eight days and nights of being team players, singing the old alma mater from ten years ago that we sing every Friday night. And Styx or REO Speedwagon or Bruce Springsteen or Journey plays loud from someone's radio. It's like being in a beer commercial.

J odi Berman is my best friend at camp. She is superathletic, and I call her Miss Soccer and Miss Softball and Miss Basketball because she always plays so hard, takes it so seriously, so that while all the rest of us are pulling up grass or stealing looks over at Boys Camp while we play, Jodi is sweating, fingers on the ball or bat, ducking blocks, hitting the softball way out into the lower field and then running as fast she can and snapping our attention back to the game. Jodi has braces, like Rachel and just about everybody else at camp, and she wears her stringy brown hair parted in the middle and clipped to either side with bobby pins. Jodi's bat mitzvah in Livingston, New Jersey, is the first I experience, and it is there I learn about the whole culture of the bat mitzvah: the big, gaudy, hysterically expensive coming-out-as-a-Jew party, the bag full of envelopes that Jodi and her parents empty onto the kitchen table after everyone leaves, checks totaling nearly fifteen thousand dollars spilling out in every direction.

I am also close to Laurel Paci, this flashy Italian girl whose religious status I can't quite pin down the whole time I'm at camp.

Are there Italian Jews? Laurel is the one in the tight pink pants, striped halter tube top, and dirty white sneakers. She is the one with the most makeup on, the dusty rose blush, the navy blue eyeliner, the super shiny lip gloss. She is the one standing at the mirror, curling iron in one hand, round brush in the other, blow-dryer tucked between her thighs, long after we are supposed to be at the rec hall for Friday-night Sing. She is the one most likely to come back to the bunk with a hickey or not to come back at all.

Laurel and I bond when we start going out with these two boys, Avi and Aaron, who are best friends. Avi is an innocent with smooth white skin, curly brown hair, and dark, easily pained eyes. Aaron could be half black, with his darker than average skin and his fuller than average lips. But his hair is straight as a board, and I am too afraid to ask him if he is black, afraid that if I ask him he might ask me and I am not sure how that would go, if he will still like me if I tell him, straight out, the simple truth.

A aron and Avi walk up to Laurel and me in the canteen, Aaron from around behind me, wrapping his arms around my waist and lifting me up, catching me by surprise. I can hear Laurel laughing next to me, can see the white and blue of Avi's leather baseball jacket. Jay glances over between boards, making eye contact with Aaron, who says, What's up, in this wannabe cool way. There is awkward joking, and Avi says something about Laurel's makeup looking like a Frankenstein mask and she brings her arm back and punches him high on the fleshy part of his shoulder, hard, so that he actually falls back a little, grabbing and massaging the spot while Laurel, reveling in her strength, laughs cruelly in his face. And then Aaron makes a face and tells a dumb joke to take the edge off, and I start laughing and then we all stand around, groping for words, movements, nonchalance, trying to pretend this isn't the moment we have all four imagined dozens of times in the course of our day, while playing softball, eating sloppy joes at the mess hall, washing Finesse conditioner out of our hair, ironing our Sergio Valente jeans: the moment when we would see our boys at the canteen, and they would see us.

Laurel says, Let's play foosball, and so we do, the four of us sidling up to the tabletop soccer game, each of us grabbing two of the eight handles. Laurel is the most aggressive, standing up on the tips of her red, white, and blue Nike Air Cortez sneakers like some kind of football-playing ballerina, putting her entire body into spinning the little men on the steel rods around and around, and knocking the heavy white ball clear across the table. When Laurel scores she looks over at Avi and Aaron and laughs mockingly, taunting them with jokes about who is going to give whom their canteen candy later. I watch us play from someplace far away and safe, watch Aaron be shy and nervous, watch Avi look around bored at the break after a goal, watch Laurel flirt with her eyes. I watch myself try to will my body into some kind of normal posture, into some semblance of ease and comfort to disguise my feeling of not belonging. I watch myself perform, shift, contort, sweat.

There are plenty of girls at camp I don't like at all, girls who whine or preen too much, girls who are cliquish and precious and so rich they think they are better than me, looking through me when I pass or speak as if I were nothing more than a piece of wood. There is Andi Hirsch, whose father owns a huge department store chain and who shows up on the first day of camp with not one but two huge trunks full of brand-new designer clothes, mix and match outfits for every possible eventuality. Andi lies on her bunk bed as I dress for a social, waiting until I am done to say something like, "Don't you think those pants are a little short?" Or, "I had that same shirt last year." She also gets care packages every week and keeps them tightly wrapped under her bed, pulling out one item at a time instead of inviting the whole bunk to a massive pig-out.

Andi is a total Jap, a Jewish American Princess, and we call her that, to her face, behind her back. Me and Pam Manela, who lives out in Queens in a big high-rise and whose parents are in clothes manufacturing, suck our teeth and roll our eyes. "She's such a fucking Jap," we spit. "Can you believe she wore real diamond earrings to camp? Uch. I hope she loses them in the lake." And then we walk arm in arm to the mess hall, splitting at the door to go to our respective tables. Jap is this word we throw around at camp, a word that is always in the air, lurking behind the gold *chai*s and purple polka-dotted Le Sportsacs, the care packages and big black trunks. We call ourselves Japs, make fun of what a "Jap camp" Fire Lake is. It means something repulsive, gauche, flashy, and yet secretly we are proud to be Japs, to think of ourselves as spoiled by Daddy's money and Mom's overprotectiveness.

When I am at camp I wear Capezios and Guess jeans and Lacoste shirts, and I assume the appropriate air of petulant entitlement. And yet I never get it quite right, never get the voice to match up with the clothes, never can completely shake free of my blackness: my respect for elders, my impatience with white-girl snottiness, the no-shit tough attitude I couldn't quite perfect back with Lisa in San Francisco but which comes to me natural as rain at Fire Lake, where it makes other girls defer to me, look up to me, fear me.

There is never any fistfighting at Fire Lake, it isn't like Pelton or New Traditions or the Bronx, where I always have to contemplate proving myself with my fists. All that has been bred out of us, but we still travel in packs and cut people down with remarks and there are still obvious leaders and even more obvious followers, though it is hard to figure out what exactly makes the difference between the two.

I am not a leader in that I have a gaggle of followers trailing along after me, but people don't mess with me much, don't call me names to my face, don't, you know, push. I am black and my past is complicated because I've lived in San Francisco and Washington, D.C., and the Bronx, and when I ask Jodi or Pam why people are sometimes quiet or reserved around me, they say that I am intimidating, which doesn't really answer my question but gives me a general idea of how I am perceived. It doesn't occur to me that intimidating might be another word for black.

S tephanie also calls me that, late at night, sitting on the wooden steps outside of Bunk Fourteen, the big log cabin at the end of the Upper Road in Girls Camp. Intimidating, precocious, old for my age, different from all the other girls. It would be late, past the one o'clock counselor curfew, and Stephanie would have just made it back to the bunk. A little tipsy, she'd be sucking hard on a Marlboro Light and rubbing her eyes, which were red and glassy. She'd be wearing skintight Levi's and white Stan Smith sneakers, a gray or burgundy Oneonta sweatshirt pulled over her enormous breasts and covering all her various gold chains: her star of David, her name chain that says *Stephanie* in curlicue letters, a diamond her father gave her when she graduated from high school.

We'd be sipping kamikazes that she'd smuggled up the hill in an old beat-up canteen, talking like schoolmates, except that I was thirteen and Stephanie was nineteen, I was the camper and she was my favorite counselor. "I made out with Dave tonight," she'd say, running her fingers through her long curly brown hair and grinning. "He's so hot, I think I'm gonna sneak over to his bunk later tonight, wanna go raid?" And then, in a sober follow-up moment, after I'd said, Sure, we could go raid, but what about John?, we'd go over the pros and cons of telling her boyfriend at college that she'd fooled around at camp. I, always the purist, thought she should tell the truth. "You're so precocious!" she'd say, and then tell me to lighten up.

A few minutes later she'd be talking about how incredible and pure and fearless Jim Morrison was, pulling out and reading from *Light My Fire,* the biography about him she read over and over that summer. After sharing a passage about an orgy "Jim" had participated in, she asked me if I had sex and I told her the truth, told her about Michael.

One year all the girls in the Lodge and Ranch vote and pick me to be Blue and Gold Sing Captain, an honor reserved for four Upper Camp girls. Sing Captain is the kind of thing you spend your whole time at camp as a lower camper dreaming about. It isn't Color War Sing, which includes the whole camp, but it's the next best thing, because you have all of Girls Camp to sing your songs, and all of Boys Camp to watch and listen. I watch every year as a different cute girl from the Ranch writes the songs, coaches the campers, and has her moment of glory on Sing Night. It isn't like I say, I want to be Sing Captain, but secretly, where I can and still be safe from disappointment, I want it bad.

After all the votes are tallied and they say I won, then some of the counselors have a meeting with Alice, and then Alice comes back and says that I can't be Sing Captain because I am too bossy, too tough, because I have this problem of needing to be in control of everything and everybody. She says she thinks that will be a problem for Sing Captain. And so the girl who has three fewer votes than I do gets it, and all my friends crowd around me and say that it isn't fair and what am I going to do, call my parents, or talk to Alice.

It is Stephanie who talks to Alice for me, and it is Stephanie who, on Sing Night when Alice announces the names of the Sing Captains, yells my name from the balcony. "And Rebecca Leventhal," she shouts with her best friend Eileen, another counselor with an open face and a big pretty smile. She knows how much it means to me and how hard I worked, even after all the shit had gone down, for my team. She doesn't care if she gets in trouble, and I think she does, because Alice looks up at her from the stage and shakes her head, and then when she finishes announcing she goes over and says something to Sy, who looks up at Stephanie and Eileen and shakes his fist.

A fter foosball we get some ice cream, soft chocolate and vanilla swirl from the ice cream dispenser behind the canteen counter, and then the four of us, Laurel, Avi, Aaron and I, walk down to the upper basketball court where people are dancing to Rod Stewart. We stand around the edges of the court, Laurel and I both staring at the other dancers inside the rectangle, focusing our eyes elsewhere to avoid the awkward question of whether or not we are going to dance.

Aaron and I end up underneath an overturned soccer goal or some other athletic object that would be on either end of a long, wide field. It is a gray rubber basinlike thing, big enough for a hundred soccer balls, with no holes. It is nighttime and there are people in our bunks, and every place we can sit together outside is lit up with floodlights designed specifically to keep us from doing what we are about to do. I don't remember whose idea it is, but I remember the ground being wet and that he gets in first and holds the thing up for me to crawl under, and then once we are both inside this shell, it is pitch black and I am thinking about bases. How many bases is he going to try for and how many bases am I going to allow? We are giggling and he is sweet and I think he asks me something about kissing, like do I have a lot of experience kissing. And I say, Some, why, do you? And he says, Some. And then we start kissing.

Aaron is the first and only boyfriend I have at Fire Lake, and even though I don't let on that his attention matters, it does. Until we start going out, I feel I am off the radar screen for the boys at camp, not even an option because I am not Jewish enough, not pretty enough, not rich enough. I feel shame but don't dare show it. Instead I carry a false pride, a toughness that sets me apart.

I don't know if my father and stepmother think about race when they look for a camp for me, but when the recruiter for the camp comes to our house, that isn't one of the questions anybody asks. We ask stuff like how many horses are in the stable and how many kids are in each bunk and what are the arts and crafts facilities. We all sit around on our brown corduroy sofa and the woman answers all of our questions without hesitation, smiling at all the right moments.

When I get there I do what I do everywhere else, I heighten

the characteristics I share with the people around me and mini-mize, as best I can, the ones that don't belong. At Fire Lake I am a Jap, but not one. I know *baruch atah Adonoi Elohainu* and love Color War, but I don't own fifty Le Sportsacs or spend the week before camp starts on a Teen Tour in Israel. I move my body like I belong but I also hold it back.

HOW MEMORY WORKS

Memory works like this: At the guard gate of an expensive hotel, I feel my breath speed up, my pulse accelerate. There is a moment when it seems I may not be let through the swinging wooden arm. For a few seconds I feel as if I am suspended in time, again the proverbial deer in the headlights. The gatekeeper checks his clipboard, makes a few calls, as I grow more and more disturbed. My thighs sweat against the cold plastic bottle wedged between them, my hands grip the brown vinyl of the steering wheel a little more tightly. My friends, sensing my discomfort, pick up on my paranoia. "Some old *white* shit," one of them says, disgusted. The other, the one who reminds me later—when I am back to myself and smiling, strolling as if without a care—that this is routine and not personal, says nothing, takes no sides, looks blankly out the backseat window.

This is how memory works: I am a woman who lives in fear of being denied. There is a mask I wear, a mask of unfazable calm. With it firmly in place, my features express serene indifference. My cheeks, eyes, lips, all are placid, welcoming, nonthreatening. I convince myself that I am at ease, that I do not live as though expecting the gate to be slammed shut at any moment. This is so true of me that my friends make fun, say that I have the least discomfort with entitlement of any young black woman they know. "Not Rebecca," they say when talking about the anger they often feel when followed in a store, about the reluctance with which they will return something inedible to the kitchen at a restaurant, about the itchy anxiety they feel in a room full of rich, well-educated white people. "She doesn't care about all that shit," they say, shaking their heads. "She just does whatever she wants, gets whatever she wants when she wants it."

And to some extent, this is true. My parents raised me to believe I am entitled to whatever is available. There is no question as to whether or not my birth or my breeding merits it. This, to counteract the idea that being black or being a woman, or being Jewish, means having to settle for less, for the thing that is not the best, for whatever it is they are trying to give you rather than what you want. This means I have the nerve to expect admittance, service, respect. At any kind of gate, be it physically real or intellectually abstract, I assume I will be allowed to enter. If detained I know with every cell in my being that I am ready to be indignant and that I will use whatever I have at my disposal, usually my words but often the law, to demand access. This, the legacy of two parents who spent a great deal of their energy fighting for it.

But memory is stronger than legacies, much stronger than principles, moral mandates, and progressive imperatives. Even though I appear "zenned out," as one friend describes me in those moments that test all of us who haven't grown up in the white ruling class, all of us who expect, at some point, to be held at the gate, interrogated and turned back, I am, in fact, trembling. This is how memory works. It reminds me that no matter how strong I feel in myself, I am still the little girl with the legs that aren't right. I am still the little girl who is too dark or too light, too rich or too poor to be trusted. Memory works like this: I am always standing outside the gate, wanting to be let in. I am always terrified that this is where I will have to live: forever wanting, never fulfilled, always outside.

And so, more often than not, I choose not to remember.

But the memory doesn't disappear. It fades from the mind I know and creeps like a parasite into my soft tissue, muscles, glands. At meetings, in stores, during interviews, at dinners and lunches with friends and family I sweat giant dark spots in powder blue shirts, and I fight a relentless urge to flee. My hands grip too tightly at steering wheels, pens, silverware. This is how memory works: I wear a mask of belonging because this is what I am supposed to do, because belonging is my birthright. But behind the mask lurks a far more mutilating truth: I am not fit, there is something wrong with me, I am not correct.

The guard at the gate tells me I do not have an appointment, the wooden lever does not swing open for me. Forgetting everything I know about gatekeepers, that they merely do the dirty work, that they are not in control, I flash into a momentary rage. I demand, bomb, maim with my eyes. My gestures are sharp, contemptuous. My words strike again and again, hitting their mark like some kind of wild beast, a stallion bucking his break.

At this largely routine checkpoint I am as close to out of my body, as close to pure rage as I can be. I take giant liberties and then, just as quickly, when I have humiliated the man at the gate to the point of surrender, when the huge, now surreal lever finally does rise to let me through, I am not victorious but ashamed. An hour later I am still fretting; I want to go back, to get on my knees and apologize, to make myself plain. I have learned again how memory works, how unsolved fragments, hurts left intact on the body fester still.

This is how memory works. Beneath the mask, behind the cool, unperturbed exterior there is rage. There is pure liquid fire threatening to annihilate. And I am afraid.

everyone in Larchmont is white every

BRONX

Yeah, so. We stand at the bus stop, waiting for the M1, which takes us down the hill, around and past all the big apartment buildings called The Century and The Premiere and The Winston Churchill, where I live. It is after school and hot and somebody has a box, and this year the big song is "Planet Rock" by Soul Sonic Force. We jam all the way down the hill on the bus, windows open, us taking over the whole long boat of the bus, yelling to old Jewish ladies pushing their grocery carts, "Rock rock to the Planet Rock, don't stop!" And Melissa is talkin' all fast like usual in Nuyorican to her sister, "Listen, girl, you'd better not tell Momi, you hear me? 'Cause she'll kill me if she knew I'm goin out with a twenty-year-old Dominican, I swear to God."

After being around her so much I talk like her, shaking my head and pushing my whole mouth forward, pursing my lips for all that attitude she picked up somewhere between San Juan, which she's never seen, and the Bronx, where she grew up. And she puts her hand on her hip and shakes her head, and her black wavy hair sways a little and her pinkish-red lip gloss shines, and a gold necklace spelling her name lies flat on her yellow neck.

This year me and Melissa both do Dominican boys, I guess because they are hot, or maybe just because they are around. I have a Dominican boyfriend on the Concourse named Ray, and I also have a crush on this boy César. He goes to the high school down at the bottom of The Hill. César is Loída's big brother and Loída is one of my friends, but she is serious about school so we don't hang with the same crowd until we get on the bus. "Yo, girl, you comin' to my house today or what?" she says, holding her fake leather briefcase with the fake gold initials.

Loída and César live in a big old building up the street from the 235th Street subway el. It has a little glass door and two elevators that don't work. A big girl named Sam lives with her mother and her crazy drinking father on the first floor. Sam dresses like a man, in big plaid flannel shirts and jeans. Her one vanity is her blond hair, which she tends with a comb whipped out of her back pocket. Sam can drink more beer, faster, than any of us, and when she's drunk she wants to fight.

Jesús lives in an identical building across the street. In the winter we all listen to music in the stairwell between the fifth and sixth floors of his building. Jesús and his girlfriend Lisa make out under the landings, groping around in the darkness there, fighting the cold. In the summer we wear tube tops and shorts and lotion our legs and hang out on the steps of Sam's building, under the streetlight, talking shit. We smoke cigarettes, Newports, and drink orange and grape soda. We eat oily slices from Vinny's Pizzeria.

I flirt with César, but he wants my best friend Theresa, who is blond and blue-eyed and thick. I am young, copper-colored, and look like his sister. He knows I like him, and sometimes runs his tongue over his lips slowly, looking me straight in the eyes, daring me. Unsure of his intent, I play it cool by laughing and lowering my lashes. The best we can do is play fight. We get physical, like Olivia Newton-John sings in a song that is popular, when he takes something of mine, like my cigarettes, and I tackle him to get them back. His stomach is smooth and warm under the football jersey he lets me wear.

One day after school it's hot and we don't have anything to do and Sam suggests we get some mescaline from a guy she knows. I don't know what mescaline is, but if we all are gonna do it, I am down. I am wearing red cotton pants and a flowery shirt, the one Melissa and I bought one day on the Grand Concourse near Alexander's. We were shopping for her name chain, looking for the cheapest one, and trying on big belts with brass name plates that spelled DARIN and ICESKI and KOOL.

Jesús, César, Theresa, Lisa, and I wait on the steps outside the building while Sam goes over to the park to buy. Jesús's front tooth is chipped and he is tall, dark, and angular. His arms are muscled, and we all suck our teeth and say he is fine and built. We call Lisa trashy, though I don't know what makes her trashier than the rest of us. Maybe it is her brother being a dope dealer and them living behind a house in a place nobody ever sees. Lisa is thick too, and her hair is feathered back from her face, and she wears tight Jordache jeans and carries a red comb in her back pocket. She feuds with Diane, Jesús's longtime ex-girlfriend who is very Católico and light-skinned Puerto Rican. Her family is straight from the Island, and strict.

We see only Diane when she comes out wheeling her sister's baby's stroller, sucking on a green-apple Blow Pop. Her name chain says *Diana*. She goes up to Jesús in front of Lisa all slow and sexy and asks him how he's doing. He practically falls over following her lips on the Blow Pop, and his body is pulled to hers, so that before he can stop himself he puts his face close and tries to talk to her in her ear and Lisa gets mad and picks up her little black purse and starts stomping toward the el. Diane laughs and leans into Jesús a little and he puts his arm around her, letting his big brown palm spread out over her butt. He pulls her to him like that and then she laughs again and tells him to remember the *niño* and she pulls away and says goodbye and winks at him as she pushes the stroller up the hill. We pretend we aren't watching. When Diane turns the corner, Jesús goes running down the hill after Lisa. In a few minutes, we look up and see them walking up from the el, holding hands. Jesús kissing Lisa's neck, making promises.

Sam comes back with the tabs. They are white or yellow, I can't remember, round, with a line in the middle. We each take one, sharing a Coke. Standing around nervously, giggling, making jokes, we wait for the drug to do something. I am the youngest. I have no idea what to expect. I walk to the curb and slide myself onto the hood of a parked car. I look up to the roof of the building and notice the decorations around the windows. I check to see that my school bag is safe by César's knee. Sam is talking about the guy that sold it to her, a friend of her brother's who lost his leg in Vietnam. I let my head fall all the way back until my eyes smack the blue of the sky. The clouds start going by fast. Soon it feels like I'm not on the car anymore and I am falling in circles into the sky. A car speeds by close to my head and I hear a bunch of guys laughing over loud music. They yell something out at us, but I think only Jesús is straight enough to give them the finger.

The mesc mixes into my blood, and after a few minutes I am peering at the others, trying to see if it is all of us or just me feeling it. We grow quieter and the cars driving by on the street get louder. Everybody starts laughing, and me too, but I can't figure out what I am laughing at, and that starts to worry me. That little bit of worry turns into some kind of ghost-baby that I watch fall down onto the ground, and when it hits the hard and dirty cement and lay there crying, on the curb, my laughter turns too. To tears. And then I am sobbing on the hood of the car, and everyone crowds around and no one is in their right mind and there is confusion and Sam gets mad and punches the hood of a car and says I shouldn't have done it.

When I start to laugh and then cry, alternately, every five minutes, and after I won't move, screaming hysterically at Jesús when he tries to take my arm and lead me inside the building, then they all get serious and huddle together. The sun starts to go down and it is cooler. I listen with half of myself, and their words blur and go right past my face not in my ears and it is only when Sam says she is going to call my father that I hear and beg her not to.

She calls Ray instead. Ray the boyfriend who works at a movie theater on the Concourse who I met at a party on the Concourse and with whom I danced pelvis to pelvis for hours. I go to the movies every Saturday after that. When his boss isn't around, Ray finds me in the darkness and we make out all over the red velour seats, twisting and arching and panting. Ray has the straightest black hair and the slyest smile. He told me he goes to Cardinal Hayes, the parochial school uptown.

We are still standing together outside of César and Loída's building when Ray comes barreling down the street in a big brown van with flames painted on the sides. From the curb I see that the steering wheel has a silver chain wrapped around it. A few baseball bats lie on the carpeted floor. Four or five guys I have never met sit inside on swivel seats. Ray jumps out of the van and rushes me, stopping his face only millimeters from mine. He grabs my shoulders and shakes me hard. I flop back and forth, a doll in his hands. Jesús and César back away. He yells at me, and wants to know where the drugs came from. Who gave them to me? Why did I take them? Where was the dealer? I have never seen him so angry, so serious. He is hurting my shoulders.

Suddenly everything starts to shift. The haze lifts and outlines fall back into places around objects. He tells me I am stupid for taking drugs. He tells me that he'll take care of it. All of my friends cower in a group a little away from us. I look up at him and say nothing. He climbs in the van and drives away. We go to Theresa's house to regroup. It is safe when her father is at work, and we sit around her barely furnished living room watching TV. César and Sam look up during the commercials and make fun of me, mimicking me laughing then crying. We don't talk about Ray. His appearance was like an apparition.

Sam calls us early the next morning when she gets home. The guy who sold her the tabs, the guy with one leg left from his Vietnam tour, the friend of her brother's, has been shot and killed. Police found his body underneath an overpass on the highway.

R iverdale is in the Bronx, only it isn't really the Bronx. The Bronx, with its liquor stores and residential bulletproofed weed-selling spots, its dusty deserted streets that look like a freshly bombed Beirut, is down the hill from Riverdale, far far away from the well-off people living in the new, freshly painted high-rises with stunning views of the Hudson, Olympic-size swimming pools, doormen in brown and gold suits, and a special three-dollar express bus to Manhattan.

My father and stepmother live just in Riverdale, but I live in Riverdale and the Bronx. Riverdale to me means Nanny and the Liebermans and shopping down on Johnson Avenue for challah for Friday-night dinner, to go with the chicken soup my step-mother makes. It means a little store that sells OshKosh overalls to my stepmother for my two-year-old brother, Ben, her firstborn son. It means walking around with my stepmother, this Sephardic-looking Jew who calls me her daughter around people who never question.

The Bronx means saying hello respectfully to Mrs. Colón

when I visit Loída or César. It means Dominican boys from JFK High School, Zulu Nation and Afrika Bambaataa, and fast girls getting pregnant young. The Bronx means being ready to fight. It means walking around with my friends Sam and Jesús and Theresa and Melissa and being seen as I feel I truly am: a Puertorriqueña, a mulatta, breathed out with all that Spanish flavor. A girl of color with attitude.

At 2500 Johnson Avenue, I take piano lessons from an old lady with hideous breath, learn "Drink to Me Only with Thine Eyes," and play it over and over before finally giving up piano for good; I go up and down on the elevator between my stepmother's mother's apartment on the tenth floor and ours on the eighteenth, carrying eggs, blankets, mandelbrot. And I babysit for the Liebermans, Rhona and David, a nice young couple with two blond boys, when they want to escape their kids for an evening and go out to dinner and a movie.

When Rhona and David leave their apartment, I play with their boys and put them to sleep before going through their books, looking for what I don't know, signs of life, some insight into who they really are. They have lots of Saul Bellow, John Updike, Norman Mailer, James Michener, Sidney Sheldon. Real men's books, I think to myself, real white men's books. What does Rhona read, I wonder, in addition to the dozens of cookbooks in the kitchen? I don't hit upon anything that even remotely interests me until I discover a stack of *Penthouse* and *Playboy* magazines in their bedroom bathroom. I put the chain on the front door, make sure the boys are asleep, and pull a few of them onto the living room sofa for a closer look.

I flip, turn the magazines sideways for a full view, try to get all the cartoons. I have never had pure, uninterrupted time with pornography and I am amazed, not only by the glossy pictures of naked women, their vaginas spread so wide and looking so wet, but also by the fact that the magazines themselves are out in plain view and not locked in a steel cabinet somewhere. I wonder if my father ever looks at magazines like these, and if he does, where he hides them because I never see one in our house. The closest my father comes to revealing his sexuality is when he tells me there is nothing wrong with looking at a beautiful woman. I wonder how it makes Rhona feel, to know that her husband takes quick trips to the bathroom to look at naked bodies that do not belong to her.

Johnson Avenue is where I get my period, running home from the bus stop with the strange wetness between my legs, an inkling of what is happening to me dawning in my stomach. I rip down my jeans in the bathroom to find the muddy red spot and then walk out into the hallway with my pants still around my knees, calling my stepmother the same way I did when I was in fourth grade calling her to see the first hair on my vagina. I tell her that I got it and she smiles and gives me some pads, and she tells me that she is excited for me. When Daddy comes home that night she tells him at the dinner table, and he smiles this embarrassed but pleased smile and I get up from the table to get some milk or to answer the phone or to get more challah from the wax bag on the counter.

The thing is that it is all fine there, at 2500 Johnson Avenue, and when I am there in it I don't question it, but I don't, ever, invite my friends over. I can't imagine where Melissa or Theresa would sit or stand in our little two-bedroom apartment. That, and also my bedroom, the one I share with my little brother, is full of REO Speedwagon and Styx records, Air Supply and Bruce Springsteen, all the records I listen to at camp, which I ordered from the Columbia Records mail-away record club. My radio is tuned to 98.7 KISS FM and I sing along with Luther Vandross, *Woke up today looked at your picture just to get me started,* but there isn't anything else in the whole apartment that looks or sounds or smells like my friends' houses, that would prove that I am of color, that I am who I say I am outside of these walls.

The only time the split is bridged is when my father drives me down the hill to Theresa's house. But even then, he doesn't come inside, he just pulls up to the front of her broken-down-looking house and asks me if I'll be okay, if I am sure I'll be okay. But I am already out the door, practically running from the white Volvo, and not turning back to watch him drive away.

And there are the times he takes me to Melissa's, out on the Concourse. He drives up to her building, one of the ones with the revolving door and the little courtyard, and he is the only white person around as far as the eye can see. He asks in that same way, Are you sure you'll be okay? And I think to myself that *I* am going to be fine, but will he? I belong because my skin says I do, because people don't question me, don't look at me and think of all the wack shit that white people do. They don't assume I have money or that I don't respect them. I can walk like I know, I can cock my head to one side and look at someone like they better step off, but

my father? I worry that he's just another white man walking down
the street, an easy mark.

One day, it has to be a Saturday 'cause the sky is so blue and
we all are laughing and joking around and dressed and not
in school, a bunch of us go to see *E.T.* at the movie theater across
the street from the rundown gift shop nobody ever goes into, on
the downtown side of the el. It is me, César, Loída, Jesús, Sam,
and some little white girl Sam is baby-sitting. We think the movie
is a joke, even though we cry when E.T. has to go back to his
planet and root for that little kid when he tries to get him to stay,
and think that baby Drew Barrymore is the cutest thing ever. It is
just that suburban house, the refrigerator filled with milk and
cookies and bologna and cheese, and those streets that look like
nobody ever walks on them that we can't quite get. Sam hates it,
says the movie is stupid, 'cause that shit wouldn't never happen.
She says those motherfuckers would've killed E.T. the first time
they saw him. Shit, she says, I would have. Fuck that. Some weird-
looking alien shit, coming 'round my house? I don't think so.

Theresa is home cleaning her house and taking care of her
crazy mother like she does every Saturday while her father works.
After the show I go to sit with her while she runs through a list of
chores as long as my arm, and that night I stay with her in that
big, empty, half-finished house with boards over the back windows and patches of loose linoleum sliding on the kitchen floor.
We listen to Chicago sing "Hard to Say I'm Sorry" over and over
while the TV blares *Let's Make a Deal* in the living room and we

feel but don't say anything about the eerie silence of her mother shut away in the room upstairs.

Out of all the days and nights I've stayed over at Theresa's, sleeping together in her little bed and smoking cigarettes on the makeshift balcony out her bedroom window, I've seen her mother only two or three times. Each time is the same. I'm up in Theresa's room, straddling the windowsill with my legs, one foot inside the bare-walled room and one foot on the tarred roof of the porch downstairs. Her mother stumbles in, knocking the door open with her cane or with her hand wrapped around a flowery glass. She stammers, "Theresa, get me some ice," or, "Theresa, where is my medicine?," or, "Theresa, your sister called, you have to go pick up Tiffany and Bobby from school."

Theresa doesn't look up from the mirror where she's blow-drying her hair. "Yes, Ma, okay, Ma," and then she looks over at me with a goofy toothy smile, rolling her eyes through the thick black eyeliner she has painted on, through the Maybelline mascara. She doesn't turn the hair dryer off either, just screams over the noise, Okay, Ma, thanks, Ma. Or if it is the curling iron, she just keeps twisting her light brown hair around the metal, flipping one section at a time for the Farrah Fawcett do that we all want but that only girls who have hair like Theresa, white-girl hair, can have.

Mrs. Androtti just stands there, one hand tugging at her faded housedress, eyebrows drawn on all wild, eyes struggling to focus from behind her cheap drugstore bifocals, until Theresa tells her to go back to her room. "Go lie down, Ma, I'll take care of it," flat a, nasal twang, loud, looking in the big mirror on the wall of her little room, pink and green mascara wands and cracked squares of blush scattered across the top of the bureau. And me in the window, watching her doing her hair, putting on her makeup, getting herself ready for the boys who'll be watching as she walks down Broadway to buy milk and laundry detergent.

I am infatuated with Theresa, content to sit at her side while she washes dishes, talks about all the boys she likes, does her biology homework from the Catholic high school she goes to, and dreams out loud about being a nurse, moving to live with her sister, and getting away from her parents. I am pulled to her, I like being the barrier between her and her father when he comes into her room barking orders. She says she can handle him, that he would never do anything to hurt her, but just the same I can tell he is on good behavior when I am around and that Theresa feels freer.

I am more comfortable at Theresa's house than I am at my own: the clean, well-lit, totally finished two-bedroom apartment up the hill with parquet floors and a view of the Hudson River and the George Washington Bridge. Her house, two boxy stories at the top of an uneven set of concrete stairs, hidden behind overgrown bushes and wild Bronx trees, reflects how I feel inside much more than the calm, collected, solidly middle-class world of my father and stepmother and their new baby boy. I am at home among the mess, the drama, the darkness of Theresa's house; there I find a corner to fit into, walls that contain me.

LARCHMONT

M y stepmother wants to live in Larchmont. I don't know at the time that it is, like, the Jewish dream to live in the suburbs, as close to Scarsdale as possible; to have a Volvo or two in the garage next to the kids' bikes and baseball gear; to eat Dannon yogurt and bagels every Sunday and light Shabbat candles on Friday night; to get a baby-sitter one night a week so that you and your husband, fresh off the six-forty train from the city, can go see the romantic comedy playing at the local uniplex. All I know is that we leave the Bronx. We pack up apartment 18J in The Winston Churchill, say goodbye to the Liebermans and my piano teacher with her horrible breath, and drive half an hour up the Cross Bronx Expressway, by way of the Henry Hudson, to a three-bedroom wooden frame house on half an acre in Larchmont.

I think that the house is very *Father Knows Best* and the move is some kind of plot my stepmother has concocted to kill me, to wipe away all traces of my blackness or to make me so uncomfortable with it that I myself will it away. I don't know that I am thinking this, but I am. I think that she and I are doing battle for my father's soul, me with my brown body pulling him down memory lane to a past more sensual and righteous, she scratching the dirt off pale Jewish roots I didn't know he had.

E veryone in Larchmont is white. What black kids there are come from the wrong side of the tracks, Mamaroneck, Larchmont's poor cousin. I don't even see them until I start school at Hommocks, the middle school at the end of a curvy drive, which on any given morning during the school year is filled with Jaguars, Volvos, and BMWs. It is not a successful integration. We all are there together but are impossibly separate. The black kids are scruffy, unkempt, ashy. They cut school, skulk through the halls, yell to one another loudly, and try in any number of other uncouth ways to assert themselves in the sea of white, rich, Jewish kids who studiously avoid them. After a few weeks at Hommocks I do the same, averting my eyes guiltily when a black kid in patched-up jeans passes me in the lunchroom, in the hallway, in class. Not once does a black student say a word to me while I am at Hommocks, not one time that whole year.

I lie outright that year. To my best friend Lauren in the downstairs bathroom, right down the brown-tiled hallway from the front doors of the school. She has just come out of one of the stalls and I am washing my hands and she asks me what am I, anyhow. She has taken a bathroom break from AP English, where they are reading *A Midsummer Night's Dream,* and I have walked out of Social Studies, where we are learning about the United Nations. I have no idea how to answer her question, though I know what information she is looking for. What am I? The black kids are scruffy, unkempt, ashy. I get really hot. I look at my feet. I wash my hands and begin to hyperventilate.

I'm Spanish, like from Spain, I say, and tear off a paper towel to put a period on it. Really, she says in a way we joke about all year, that way Lauren has of saying *really* that is dorky and weird and sounds like her nose had grown lips. Reelly? And I say yes, and she never asks me about it again, not even when there is a big article in the newspaper about my mother, lauding her as a big African-American writer and mentioning that she has a daughter, this half-Jewish half-black girl living with her father in Larchmont.

I hate Larchmont. I hate how quaint and provincial it is, that everybody seems to know each other, that there are only two pizza places and one grocery store and one junior high. I hate that everybody is white, that when I walk down the street people look at me funny, as if I don't belong. I hate that Larchmont is not the Bronx, where all my friends are, and I hate that my father is choosing this totally bourgeois lifestyle that makes me puke, and that I'm forced to choose it along with him even though a picket fence is not my idea of happiness.

There is something about the way the houses are, all in a row with their little plots of lawn out front, the way at dusk men and women in black and gray and navy blue suits start filling the streets, walking home from the train station. There's something too predictable about the patterns of life here, as if they're drawn on rather than actually lived. It makes me sick.

A llison Hoffman's house is smooth gray stone and glass and from the outside looks like it should be in an architectural magazine, all straight lines and flat planes shooting out from each other. I have never seen a house as fancy this close-up, but I pretend not to notice, letting my eyes skip over the manicured lawn out front, the Mercedes and Jaguar in the car port. Allison and I walk up to the house from the direction of our school, which is at the other end of a windy road lined with puffy beige grasses and a little fake lake. The sky is a sparkling blue, and the air is chilly but not quite cold.

When we step inside her house an older Latina woman in a black-and-white maid's uniform comes to the door and takes Allison's book bag and coat. When she does, Allison says to her in this fake nicey nicey voice, "Thank you, Maria," and then smiles that smile I have seen her smile at people she's not really friends with but who she knows she should be nice to anyway. Then Maria asks if we want anything to eat. Do we want sandwiches, cookies, juice, crackers? Allison answers in the same sing-songy voice, but this time a little too firm and dismissive I think for someone our age to say to a woman so much older, "No thanks, Maria, we can get something ourselves."

I feel embarrassed when Allison talks this way to Maria, and especially when Maria looks at me cautiously before walking away. For a moment I feel closer to Maria than I do to Allison, like I should call her Mrs. Somebody and I should go with her to the kitchen or wherever she's walking to, and not stay back here in the fancy front rooms with Allison.

But I do stay in the front rooms with Allison, nodding and trying not to look impressed by everything she's showing me. First it's the sliding glass doors off the living room and the pool they lead to. Then it's the library, with its multiple sets of encyclopedias, big leather chairs, and colorful globe. Then it's her parents' bedroom, where everything is matching gray and beige, with a big television and identical phones on either side of the bed. Then it's her brother's room, with its Lacrosse sticks propped against the wall, and blond women in bathing suits tacked up over his dresser.

As I look around her house and listen to her talk about shopping for her upcoming bat mitzvah, how huge her brother's was a few years before, and how we should watch some videos before her violin teacher comes to give her a lesson, I chatter along with her, keeping it light, trying to match her rich, carefree frequency. I tell her that I'm not having a bat mitzvah because I haven't been to Hebrew school, and when she asks me what San Francisco is like I tell her it's really beautiful, with fog and hills and lots of roller skating in the park. When she asks me about Riverdale I tell her about how close it is to the city and that my bedroom had like, an amazing view of the Hudson River and the George Washington Bridge.

While I'm talking Allison makes little faces, nodding and squinching up her mouth and her nose until she looks like a mouse. Then she pulls her wavy brown hair in and out of its ponytail holder, fussing with it in a distracted way, like what I'm saying isn't quite capturing her attention. When she does that I try to imagine Allison hanging out with César, Loída, and Sam. I try to imagine her in the Victorian frame house I live in, in my small room with the box fan and slatted wooden floors and flowery sheets my stepmother bought on sale at Bloomingdale's. I feel as if we speak two different languages and I am the only one who can speak both, who even knows that there is more than one to be learned.

A llison is one of the girls I talk about when Theresa comes to my house to visit, after her new police-officer boyfriend drives up in an old faded blue Plymouth to drop her off. It's late and we've made a pallet on the floor next to my bed out of some old quilts and a comforter. We're both lying down there, fiddling with the knob on my stereo, trying to tune it to WPLJ, and gossiping about who's going out with who back in Riverdale. She tells me that Jesús and Diane are back together, César is going out with this girl who is older than him and really pretty, and Loída finally has a boyfriend but he's a total nerd.

It's strange having Theresa at my house since it's always been the other way around, I'm always the one going into her world, she's never coming into mine. She seems out of place in my room, and even more so sneaking downstairs in the middle of the night to eat the rest of the Entenmann's chocolate chip cookies hidden in the bottom drawer of the refrigerator. It's a bit of a shock to see Theresa in a kitchen that's well lit and full of shiny white Formica. She looks different juxtaposed against it, faded, haggard, and slightly green. I notice the concealer caked under her eyes, her long pink nails, her fake-looking blow-dried hair.

When Theresa asks me about my friends here, when she asks me what the other kids are like, I tell her about Allison, about Allison's house and Allison's maid. I tell her that Allison wouldn't last five minutes at 141 with her uppity attitude. She'd get her ass kicked. I laugh with Theresa as I say this but in the pit of my stomach I feel some guilt, like I am betraying Allison, choosing sides because it's convenient. After Theresa leaves I am exhausted but relieved. I love her but it is too hard to be the translator, the one in between, the one serving as the walkway between two worlds.

Tina and I are at Dark Star Records, and Shawn is playing the Clash up front while we stack quarters up on the Centipede game in the back. Shawn is from England and he opened Dark Star just a few months before I got to Larchmont. He's got pasty white skin, a pointy nose, and a mass of dark frizzy hair. He always wears the same thing, tight skinny-legged blue jeans with pointy black shoes and a multicolored pullover sweater. When we're in the store, he plays Flock of Seagulls, Modern English, the Clash, and the Who. He plays Duran Duran at our request, turning his back in disgust as we sing along at the top of our lungs to "Rio."

Dark Star is the black sheep of Larchmont, the freaky, out-of-place thing that isn't like all the others on Sesame Street. As it is, it's next to Eggemoggin, the tchotchke store, where Tina and I go to buy presents for birthday parties, picking and choosing from teddy bear stickers, edible face paint, and monogrammed pastel stationery. I don't know what possessed Shawn to open Dark Star in Larchmont, but I feel close to him; he, too, is a foreigner.

When Tina and I are out of quarters and our fingers hurt from shooting fluorescent spiders, we hang over the counter and listen to Shawn talk about the punk scene in London. He tells us about Sid Vicious, about all the boys wearing bright orange mohawks and the Union Jack safety-pinned to their black leather jackets. When Tina and I make a music video in Media Arts class, it is Shawn's influence that comes through as we strum on borrowed guitars. In our best British urban ghetto cool, Tina and I prance around the tiny stage in the Media Arts lab, lip-synching the words to our favorite Police tune, "Every Little Thing She Does Is Magic," and flirting with the camera.

Tina is my best friend here and she's flipping her straight dirty-blond hair over her shoulder in between boards as she plays, but it creeps back and then she has to ask me to hold it for her, to keep it out of her eyes as she clears the hard board of the red Centipede that falls fast as light from the top of the screen. We're having a tournament with some boys that came with us after school to play: Paul Mangione, Brendan Ryan, Tommy Handler. It's me and her against all of them, and we're winning because we play Centipede after school every day here at Dark Star, and they don't.

We're also waiting for Luca, Tina's brother, to come meet us after hockey practice like he said he would. He said he'd meet us around four-thirty, and it's already five. Even though I'm focused on my game, I can't help but look up at the front of the shop every time the door swings open, half expecting to see Luca walk in wearing his faded army jacket that smells like patchouli, the goofy grin across his angular face that means he got stoned with his friends on the way. The other half of me is expecting to be disappointed.

Luca's being Tina's brother makes making out a lot easier because I am always at Tina's house. Our parents make jokes that I should move in I'm over there so much, that I'm the Nastris' long-lost daughter from Sicily. The truth is I love Tina's roomy house, the way all the kids have floors of their own, the way the parents' room is far enough away from us kids that we can do anything, make any amount of noise without them hearing. At Christmas, the Nastris put up a huge tree and fill the house with Perugina chocolates. At dinner the whole family talks about stuff going on in school, and the kids get to be flip and sarcastic without the world coming to an end.

Luca's room is at the top of a little narrow staircase that's almost secret. His room is small and always smells like a mixture of pot, his dirty hockey uniform, and the patchouli oil he buys in the city. It is always cold in his room, and dark. He has Clash posters on the wall, dirty beat-up Saucony sneakers on the floor, rank and faded jeans in a heap by the bathroom door.

The most exciting thing about Luca Nastri, in addition to the fact that he's cute and a renegade, is that he goes to the *high school*. I'm in eighth grade and I'm going out with a boy from the high school. That means I get to go to high school games and wear his hockey jersey. That means some days I wait for him to come and pick me up at Hommocks when he's done with hockey practice. That means a lot of the girls in my grade look at me different, with a kind of grudging respect. Except for the stuck-up snotty girls who think that the stoner crowd, Luca's crowd, is gross and dirty. But I don't give a shit about them.

L uca Nastri is the first boy I give a blow job, down under the mussed-up tangled sheets in his bed, after we've taken a few bong hits and made sure that Tina and her parents are asleep. We've been making out for a while and Luca has been holding my tiny breasts in his cold hands, kneading them in a way that doesn't feel good but that I tolerate because I don't know yet that I can say, Hey, that doesn't feel good, this would feel better. And we're lying like that, in his bed, stoned and giddy and slightly para-noid, when he takes my hand and pulls it down to his penis, which is straining against the white cotton of his Fruit of the Loom briefs.

I'm fascinated. I squeeze it and pull it out from his belly, amazed by the way it snaps back when I let it go. After I press against it with my fingers a couple more times and feel it jerk back in response, I reach under the waistband and wrap my palm around his hard, smooth, perfect dick, and then, before I know it, Luca is pushing me down toward it and then he asks me to lick it, and I say, Lick it? And he says, Yeah, and so I do, with little tiny strokes like a lollipop until he pushes the whole thing into my mouth and puts his hand on the back of my neck and then I am sucking and tasting the salty whiteness dribbling out the top and feeling strong and powerful but also nervous and unsure.

After Luca comes, pulling out of my mouth just in time to shoot wildly into a dirty, balled-up tee shirt, he pulls me close to him and tells me that it was great, that he really liked it and did I.

I say yes even though part of me wonders, is that it? And another part of me wonders, did I do it right, or is he just saying that? But I don't say anything out loud, I am happy to be lying in his arms where it is warm and I feel for one second like I belong, like Larchmont isn't quite as bad as I thought.

Even after Luca falls asleep and I am lying in his arms, I hold on to that feeling, not wanting to let it go. I am the chosen one, I think. I am in Luca's bed, in his arms, I am inside, not out; I am the one being stayed with, not the one being left. I am not just alone, out in the world, fending for myself.

I don't tell my father too much about Luca, and he doesn't ask. My father gets up in the morning to 1010 WINS on the radio, showers, shaves, and puts on a suit, blue or brown in the winter, light blue or beige in the summer. My stepmother drives him to the station and me to school, my new baby sister and brother strapped into car seats on my right and left in the backseat as we ride. I don't see my father until dinner time, or right before I go to bed. When I do see him, Daddy is tired, checked out, sagging. After eating chicken soup or pot roast or broiled chicken, he sits in a chair in the living room, rubbing his temples, his feet and legs heavy on the floor beneath them. Or he stretches out with a book, a biography of Gandhi or Niebuhr's *Moral Man and Immoral Society*, on the big brown sofa. I'm clearing the table or doing homework, loading the dishwasher or reading a story by Flannery O'Connor.

When we do talk for a few minutes before I go to sleep, we talk about his work or about how his back hurts. He asks me cursory questions about school and engages me a little on the one night I tell him I think Larchmont is too white. He asks me to elaborate, and when I do, tells me that some lawyer friend of his, Jim Hargood, who is black and has kids and lives in Larchmont, says he never has any problems and neither do his kids. I nod but can't help wondering what Jim Hargood's experience has to do with me. When I persist, he insists that I am fine, that I have friends and that this school is much better than the one in the Bronx. When I tell him that I'm miserable he tells me I'm exaggerating.

My father and my stepmother know I'm going out with Tina's brother, but they don't ask too many questions about what that means, going out. They don't ask what we do on the nights I spend at Tina's, they don't ask if I'm having sex or giving blow jobs or feeling safe. Back in fourth grade my stepmother told me about how babies were made, what sex is, and what a period is, and I guess she and my father think my mother has filled me in on the rest while I was with her in fifth and sixth grades. It suits me fine, I guess, this having a whole life they don't know about, moving around, making decisions without the benefit of their opinion, except that I feel so alone and unsure of myself, like I'm winging every decision, every move, every day, faking like I know what I'm doing all the time rather than being sure.

When my father tells me I'm exaggerating about my feelings about Larchmont, I want to kill him, but more than that I want to kill my white, holier-than-thou, perfect Jewish stepmother, because I'm convinced this whole place is her dream and not his, and because I'm convinced if it wasn't for her my father would still be mine and would listen to me and would tell me to be proud of who I am, that I was born for a reason and that being black and white is better than being just one thing and screw people who can't deal.

When Luca walks into Dark Star with his Italian army jacket open and the bones of his collarbone sticking out in front of him, my stomach flips and I start to sweat. He says hello to Shawn and the two of them talk about the Clash for a minute, is that new record coming in. I can tell that Luca is high because his eyes have that tight, glossy look they get when he smokes pot, and his smile is sloppy and super wide. He walks to the back of the store where I am standing with his sister and puts his arm around me, right off. I can smell him, and when he turns his lips to me I give him mine and we kiss. Then he is trying to get me to go home with him, devising ways we can convince our parents to let me and Tina have a sleepover on a school night. The last time we did that Luca and I cut school the next day and spent the morning fooling around and the afternoon walking in the woods behind his house. Everything was white and pristine because it had just snowed and the trees were dripping icicles. We rolled around on the powdery mounds, sticking our tongues in each other's mouths, feeling the wet and warm contrast with the bitter dry cold.

With one hand on the rolling ball for direction and the other tapping against the flashing button to fire, Tina asks Luca about something she heard the boys on his hockey team said about me. She heard from Jennie Hauser's brother that the team had some problems with his choice of girlfriend. When she says this Luca's face falls a bit. He reaches up and pulls the hair that has fallen out of his eyes and looks at his sister's back, avoiding my eyes. Fuck them, he says. But Tina doesn't stop. Did you tell *them* that, she wants to know. I don't want to talk about it, he says with a dead calm, and then she lets it go.

I don't hear about this again until the day Luca breaks up with me, abruptly, out of the blue, about a week after Tina told me some of his friends on the hockey team had razzed him for going out with a black girl, or, as they put it, going out with a nigger. I had gone to a hockey game, and when Luca's team won I screamed and screamed and ran up to him, wrapping my arms around his neck and laughing. I felt a few of the stares from the boys and the way Luca's body tensed up a little, but I didn't think about it. I had heard that there was some discussion at the high school about me wearing Luca's jersey around school, but I hadn't paid much attention to that either. I did freak a little when Luca told me that his coach singled him out and told him not to have sex before the game, but I thought that was some strange macho bullshit, a guy thing rather than anything to do with the color of my skin.

After Luca breaks up with me, Tina gets really mad and says that all his so-called friends suck and that her brother is a total coward, but it doesn't help. I don't tell anyone about what happens between Luca and me, not my father or stepmother, not any of the friends from the Bronx that I no longer keep in touch with. I can't imagine calling Melissa or Loída to tell them some hockey-playing boy from northern Italy dumped me because I am not white. The last time I called Melissa she asked if my house was big and if all the kids at my school had their own cars. I briefly consider calling Sam, who I know will offer to beat Luca up.

Instead I keep my hurt to myself.

Ten years later I take the train back to Larchmont from Manhattan to attend a bridal shower for my once best friend Lauren. When I pull up to the house in my father's old Volvo I am thirteen again and coming over to Lauren's to watch U2 videos on MTV, play Phoenix on her Atari, and stay up half the night talking with her sister about boys and how she hates her mother. The house is mostly the same, full of books and art, Lauren's mother's downstairs lair filled with papers and manuscripts, a computer and desk now dominating one whole side of a room. Upstairs in Lauren's room, an amber-colored bottle of Ralph Lauren perfume is still on her old white lacquer dresser, and the single bed is still pressed against the yellow wall.

I haven't seen Lauren in years but when I do see her, after pushing through the throng of chatty mostly middle-aged Jewish women I don't know, she looks exactly the same. Same curly brown hair, same slender fingers and perfectly clean natural-looking nails. Same dewy brown eyes and big open smile. Same slightly awkward posture, same arms around me, same tall white woman looking down at me with love and hope. She's nervous about seeing me, she says, do I hate her because she's getting married? You were so protective of me, she says. I pause for a moment, surprised. I *had* been shocked and a little skeptical when I heard Lauren was engaged, but hating Lauren was never an option. Before I can say that to her, though, another guest pulls at her elbow and then she's off playing princess for somebody else.

It isn't until I watch Lauren opening her presents—a shiny white Cuisinart, some purple-and-black lingerie, a cookbook filled with recipes "to keep your Jewish husband happy and home"— that I begin to remember just how protective of Lauren I was. There was a boyfriend from a mob family I had been extremely concerned about, a girlfriend who had treated Lauren badly and whom I had called one night on Lauren's behalf, there were fights with her sister that I coached her through, and long, emotional phone conversations about her conflicts with her parents.

The next morning as I walk to the station, a well-groomed man in a sweatsuit jogs alongside me, peering into my face as he passes. He goes to the corner, stops, turns around, and comes back to where I am walking. He knows my name. I am surprised. I don't expect anyone in Larchmont to remember me. But it's Chris O'Shea, and he does. He remembers that some girls at the high school were picking on him and I offered to beat them up, standing with him one day after school on the day they were supposed to come. He remembers that I never acted like I was from Larchmont, that I had all this city attitude from living in the Bronx that made me stand out. He says I was real mature, real protective, that he thought of me as a big sister. Chris O'Shea has not crossed my mind once since I left Larchmont, but now, all of a sudden this clean-cut banker is in front of me, a thick gold chain around his neck the only thing left from the days we went to school together, and I see him the way he was, loping down the halls at school with his greasy brown hair and puppy dog eyes, his gloves with the fingers cut out, his tattered winter coat and black boots with the laces spilling out.

Chris was one of those fuck-up kids, the ones who try but never get it quite right, the ones who always seem a little slow, who nod while you talk but can't really repeat back what you just said. He drank in the eighth grade, and carried bottles of alcohol his older friends bought for him in the pockets of his ripped-up trenchcoat. He chain-smoked Marlboros or Camels, they might even have been Newports. His fingers were chewed down below the cuticle and always bleeding. One day at lunchtime Chris told me that his father beat him, and he lifted up his coat and showed me welts. Another day he told me that his father hadn't let him in the house and he spent the night in the tool shed.

I always liked Chris, I would look at his eyes and his fingers and his back and soften, wanting my wing to be bigger and stronger so that he could find some shelter under it. But he was like a security blanket to me too, in all his brokenness, a kindred wandering spirit to keep me warm.

On the train back to the city, it occurs to me that I needed someone to take care of me back in eighth grade, and instead of asking for that I gave it to others, convinced that by protecting them, by wrapping my little arms around them, I could make them mine forever.

ly mother, thank God, says, okay,
we'll look my mother, thank God, says
okay, we'll look my mother, than
God, says, okay, we'll look my mother
thank God, says, okay, we'll look m
mother, thank God, says, okay, we'
look my mother, thank God, says
okay, we'll look my mother, than
God, says, okay, we'll look my mothe
thank God, says, okay, we'll look m
mother, thank God, says, okay, we'
look my mother, thank God, says
okay, we'll look my mother, than
God, says, okay, we'll look my mothe
thank God, says, okay, we'll look m
mother, thank God, says, okay, we'
look my mother, thank God, says
okay, we'll look my mother, than
God, says, okay, we'll look my mothe

I don't always make choices the standard way, the way people nowadays call healthy. I don't, at every crossroads, weigh the options, measure the odds, check my schemata to see how x or y fits. I stand at the fork waiting to be pulled by a force stronger than psychology, more precise than logic.

My sister is now seventeen and, having been admitted to Yale, waits with her classmates at their expensive northeast private high school for the world to shift. I play the part of the proud sister well, reading over her essays, attending school plays, gossiping about boys, and looking over the Eurail route scheduled for summer.

And yet as I watch her move through my father and stepmother's Upper East Side apartment, already too big for the space, already her body crying out for a dorm room all to herself, full of old newspapers and fashion magazines, Janson's big *History of Art* book and Shakespeare's sonnets, I feel a certain sadness as I ponder a life with far less uncertainty than my own. A life in which one year without interruption follows the next and goes basically according to plan: the bigger school up the street in the suburban village, the next size up at Bloomingdale's, the next chapter in a script that has, if not in fact then certainly in the cultural imagination, been written already.

I think of my own blank naivete, applying to Yale because a friend urged me to, not knowing anything much about the place, expecting when I arrived to really study the Great Books as the catalogue advertised but finding instead only those written by a small group of dead white males. I think about my own circuitous route, the bouncing from city to city, the gratitude I feel that I made it to Yale in spite of all the other holes I could have instead fallen into: drugs, juvenile hall, abusive boyfriends, unwanted children.

I make a hundred choices every day, decisions about where to put my money, who to talk to, what food to eat. And yet the fundamental experiences which have shaped my life, the cities I've lived in, the family I've been born into, the people I've been attracted to, the color of my skin, the books I am drawn to read, the ideas which compel me, none of these I choose. I find my map without a traditional trajectory, too fragmented for a linear narrative. There is always a direction. There is never a dead end, never a path that does not make me more a human being than I was before. I am always moving. I am always in life, walking.

SAN FRANCISCO

I leave Larchmont in a rage. I have literally pushed my stepmother into a mirror, cursed her to her face, and all but stopped speaking to my father. At the end of the school year I pack my bags and put them out on the front porch. I sit next to them, the old green army duffel with my name in block letters down the side in red nail polish, and an old beige nylon garment bag my mother gave me, until my father comes to drive me to the airport. He steers the Volvo down the Boston Post Road and onto the 95 highway. As everything goes by me in a rush, first the quaint little houses and then the car dealerships, gas stations, and fast-food restaurants, I tell him that I don't want to live with him anymore. I tell him I hate Larchmont, I hate Judy. I hate him. I vow never to set foot in his house again.

But we go along as if my tears and anger are the most natural things in the world. He talks about how happy I will be to see my old friends in San Francisco, not one of whom he can name. He drives to the airport as if we're going no farther than Yankee Stadium or to visit Grandma in Brighton Beach. I imagine he's look-

ing forward to a break from me and my wars with his wife, my
fights with my little brother, the way I complicate the family. In
the Larchmont Baskin-Robbins I have overheard a woman mar-
veling at what a young but capable nanny I am. Walking with my
brother and sister down Larchmont Avenue or Chatsworth, I have
been asked if I am the baby-sitter, the maid, the au pair. I imagine
that my father would like to relax and enjoy his assimilated all-
white family without the aberration, the dark spot in an otherwise
picture-perfect suburban life.

As I stare out the window crying, my father is his usual con-
strained self. What emotion he feels is buried beneath a rigid,
lawyerly mask. His response is mild, understated. "It can't be that
bad, Rebecca," and "You feel that way now, but you won't always." When we are almost to the airport and I can see airplanes
taking off and landing in the humid, overcast sky, he reaches over
and pats my leg like he has since I was a little girl, cupping his
hand slightly to make a hollow, musical sound. And then I am at
the curb in front of the airline, standing with my bags. And then
I am inside the airport, walking alone to the gate.

I enter my life in San Francisco with a vicious attitude. I slam
doors, talk back to my mother, roll my eyes, and stay in my
room all day with the door shut and music up. I am resplendent
with teenage affect. But my mother doesn't see it that way. She
wonders aloud where all this anger is coming from and shrinks
from me as if I'm covered in shit. She says I must have picked up
these bad habits from my stepmother. Maybe she was too permis-
sive. She suggests I get myself together, stressing that I won't be in-

dulged the way that I have been. Is she making a distinction between black and white parenting? Between the suburbs and the city? One morning she ventures that perhaps I have anger at my stepmother that I am directing at her. I can't say, Maybe I have anger at you that I am directing at you. I can't say, I hate all this moving and losing and trying to find home and saying goodbye.

I don't complain. That is part of the deal. Slowly I try to curb myself, to retrain myself to my mother's expectations. I am bright Rebecca, cheery Rebecca, helpful and independent to a fault. I do all of our laundry as I have from fifth grade, lugging brightly colored pillowcases full of dirty clothes down the cement walkway to the laundry room. I clean the house, scrub the tubs and toilets, and vacuum the carpets. I leave her loving goodbye notes when she leaves for the weekend or for the week to write in "the country," where it is more quiet. If I act up or forget to do what's required or make too much noise when she's working, I find a letter waiting for me on the dining-room table. In it I am chided for being selfish, inconsiderate, thoughtless, lazy. She reminds me that it is hard being a single parent, that she works hard to keep us going and that my job is to take care of myself as much as I possibly can. To avoid making demands, to avoid having needs she may or may not be able to meet.

In interviews my mother talks about how she and I are more like sisters than mother and daughter. I am game, letting her sit in my lap for a photo for *The New York Times,* playing the grown-up to my mother's child for the camera. I feel strong when she says those things, like I am much older and wiser than I really am. It's just that the strength doesn't allow for weakness. Being my mother's sister doesn't allow me to be her daughter.

In keeping with her philosophy of sisterly independence, my mother doesn't find a high school for me. She doesn't ask around or call the school board, she doesn't go around to different schools trying to see which one is the best for me. I decide to attend George Washington because Lena does and it's where her father teaches. It's also the school Michael, my boyfriend from sixth grade, graduated from. Even though it's out of my district and a forty-five-minute bus ride away, it's the only high school I know about firsthand, the only one that has a name and a face.

Washington is a huge high school, the kind you see in movies. Out back is a football field with *Washington Eagles* painted in the center and bleachers stacked on either side. Out front is a sand-colored set of concrete stairs leading to three brown double doors. The halls are lit with fading fluorescents, and the floors are shiny from the man with the waxing machine who buffs them at the end of every school day. Every hour and fifteen minutes a bell rings and students flood out of the classrooms and into the hallways. We go north or south, east or west down the corridors, and use the stairwells at the either end to go up or down. My homeroom is on the second floor, geometry is on the third, English is in the annex out back, behind the track where everybody smokes weed at lunchtime.

Even though Lena lives right down the lane and her father drives her to the same school every morning, I don't ride with them. To get to George Washington High School I walk to the corner and take the 38 Geary all the way to the Avenues, almost to Ocean Beach. I am up and out of the house before my mother wakes up. When I peek into her room to say goodbye, the shutters are closed and it's dark but I can see her head on the pillow, her blue flannel nightgown reaching almost to her neck, her forearm draped over her eyes and forehead. I don't ever eat breakfast, don't ever listen to the radio in the morning to find out the weather. I get up, pull on the jeans I ironed the night before, put my red Trapper Keeper notebook in my book bag, and double-lock the door behind me. In San Francisco I am unbearably lonely.

At Washington, Michael precedes me. Thick muscular boys sidle up next to me in the hallways and outside on the walkway in front of the auditorium. "You Michael's girl?" they ask, their dark eyes needling into my breasts, hips, and butt. "He didn't tell us about you," they say, looking jokingly at each other. "You must have been his little secret." Girls corner me in the downstairs bathroom, the one with the ceiling covered with wet tissue wads, dripping from peeling paint like icicles. "She ain't even that cute," they say loud enough for me to hear. "Mike must be having vision problems." And then they burst out laughing. When I ask Michael about these girls later, about Monique and Mayesha and Keiko and all these other San Francisco ghetto girls, he tells me which ones he's slept with, which one is just jealous, which one I have to watch out for because she likes to fight.

Every day around my neck I wear my gold chain that says *Rebecca* and about once a week I wear Michael's old football jacket, the one that has his name embroidered above my left breast. Instead of a song being "awesome" and a bad situation being "beat," at Washington it is "live" or "bunk" or some other word I pick up from my best friend Maya. Instead of tilting my head from side to side and keeping the rest of my body still, for emphasis I swivel my neck around, push my chin out, or rest my hands on my hips when I talk. Even though I still say "like" quite a bit, at Washington I only slip it into sentences at the beginning and maybe the end, instead of stringing it throughout. At Washington I say "uh huh" a lot more, and "mmhmm," pressing my lips together into a knowing smirk.

M aya and I have switchboard for third period and so from ten-thirty to eleven forty-five we sit next to each other with headsets on, pulling old brass plugs from one connection hole and sticking them in another. "George Washington High School, may I help you?" we both say, sometimes in unison if two calls come in at the same time. "George Washington, can I connect you?" Maya has a definite style with the callers. She's smooth, sometimes sickly sweet and phonily accommodating, rolling her eyes the second the caller is off the line. It's hard for me to be fake, to put it on. I'm more blunt, keeping my voice low and calm, real. "George Washington, can I help you?" Maya is a dark honey brown, with big brown eyes and shoulder-length permed hair that curls under at the ends. She paints her nails a brownish red as we sit at the switchboard. When we meet I notice Maya's nails right off, and her white teeth. A little later I notice her figure, her full hips and thighs accentuated by the tight jeans she wears, the breasts much larger than mine hidden behind lacy burgundy and beige bras I see when I spend the night at her house or when we have to change together for gym, which we both hate.

At least once a week we get a call from the same freak: this guy who likes to tell us how big his dick is and to ask us if we want to suck it. Maya just laughs at him. She's like, "Please, really now, why would I want to do that? I'm sure it's not even as big as my little brother's pinkie finger." Or she might ask him why he doesn't have anything better to do with his time. Don't you have a job? she'll ask, looking up at the big clock above our heads. It's eleven o'clock in the morning, shouldn't you be at work? For Maya he's a harmless joke but he makes me a little nervous. His voice is low and I can picture him sitting in his darkened room, frantically jerking off as he pictures us, two pretty young girls. Does he know where we are? Can he see us through the big window behind our switchboards?

Maya has been seeing the same guy since junior high school, Derek. He's who she lost her virginity to, the boy she plans on marrying. He lives down the street from her and goes to Balboa, one of the other big public schools in the city, the one out toward where she lives. Her parents know him and she knows his whole family and when I go over to her house, Derek comes over and brings a friend, usually one of his buddies from the basketball or football team and we all four hang out in Maya's linoleum-lined basement, listening to music and playing cards: Tonk or Spades.

Even though I know Maya and Derek have had sex, no one else in her family suspects, not even Karen, her older sister who knows everything. Maya's family isn't strict exactly, but her parents are from the South and have been married for thirty years. They go to church and talk a lot about what is respectful and what is not. So when we listen to songs like "Second Time Around" and "With This Ring" by Shalimar, and Derek, with his athletic red-bone body, pushes up against Maya while she's standing behind the little Formica bar pouring soda from one of those fat two-liter bottles, I'm not surprised that Maya looks at him like he's just sprouted a third arm and tells him to control himself and that he's tripping. He's in her parents' house, she reminds him, and nothing like that can happen here, whether they're home or not.

When football season starts, Michael comes up to school for the games, standing up in the bleachers in black jeans and a gray Members Only jacket while I play cheerleader down by the field, swinging pom-poms and stamping my feet to sassy Washington chants. When I sneak a look up at him and catch him staring down at me, my stomach does flips and I swear I can smell his cologne from a hundred yards away. While I scream and split and clap my hands to the beat of the accompanying marching-band drum, I close my eyes and think of Michael's tongue in my mouth, his dark strong body pressed against mine on the nights he sleeps over when my mother is away. When I open them again he is looking right at me and grinning, his big white teeth practically glowing. I rush through my cheers, gloating as I imagine Monique's face when she sees me getting into Michael's old beat-up gray Datsun.

While Michael is up visiting at the "Wash House," as we call it, he tells his friends "the fellas" to watch out for me. That means that all the guys who have been sniffing around me now have to pretend to be my big brothers, to pretend to be looking out for me instead of trying to sleep with me. A few of them keep a respectful distance, like big-ass Mark who is dark and lumbering and weighs at least 310, and Donnell who's a solid 280 and has all the girls after him on account of his big sexy athlete's body and his goofy hundred-watt smile. And even Anthony, Mr. Wanna Be Player himself, doesn't mess with me except to call me his "little sis" and ask me how "Mike" is. "How's my boy?" he'll say, hooking his arm around my neck and pressing his greasy Jheri-curled hair a little too close to my cheek. "Is he treatin' you right?"

Those guys, the older ones just a year behind Michael, they're okay. It's the younger guys who don't know Michael as well and feel less allegiance to him that are a little trickier, a little more forward. Before the end of September, Tony Hernandez, Andre Long, and Len Black all get my number without Michael finding out. Even though none of them talks about it, none of them says I'm biracial or mixed or black and white or this and that, the fact is that each of them is half black and half something else close to if not white, and each of them looks like he could be my brother.

By November, Len and I are holding hands at school and sneaking kisses out in the back field. By January, Tony and I have flirted with the idea of going out but decided we're better off as friends. By April, I'm going to Andre's wrestling matches with him and his godfather, Mack, who, with his repressed rage and cocky swagger, reminds me of a black John Wayne. I know it's serious early one Saturday morning as I stand in a cold high school gym proudly eyeing Andre's muscular, coppery-brown shoulders and thighs as he strides across the floor in his skimpy wrestling-cum-gladiator uniform.

Andre is fine. Finer than any boy I've ever liked or gone out with, and even though he knows Michael and so is off-limits, I can't help myself. Andre's room is in the garage of his mother's house, out in Ocean View, by San Francisco State, up the street from where Tony and Maya live. There aren't any windows in his

freezing cold garage room, but squares of mirrors pasted up everywhere: on the ceiling, the wall. Over his queen-size bed there's a
photograph of a dark-skinned woman lying naked on her stomach with her butt front and center. When I tell Andre I think the
photograph is offensive and degrading, he laughs. Don't I think
she's beautiful, he asks, and I can't deny it. It's just that I feel in-
adequate as I measure myself against the woman in the picture. I
can't possibly compete, not just with her easy sexuality and well-
toned thighs, but with her undeniable blackness: the dark chocolate skin, the perfectly formed thick behind.

To take the pressure off I shift my attention to something less
loaded: a photograph of Andre's father, a mirror image of a young
Marvin Gaye, complete with soulful brown eyes and strong, sharp
features, smiling down from a spot on the wall. Andre tells me
that his father died when he was young, that he doesn't remember
him too well, and then we don't mention it again, even though I
want to ask a lot more questions, like how did your parents meet
and was there any trouble because he was black and she was white.

But Andre changes the subject and we don't talk about any of
that, not until we're much older, and even then Andre shrugs it
off. "I'm African," he says years later when we are both in college
and he is explaining the work he is doing with the All African Peo-
ples Revolutionary Party and I'm raising my eyebrows at their
retro position on interracial dating. "I'm African, and so are you,"
he says to me, with his arms around my waist in my mother's
kitchen.

He's been showing me how to peel garlic by mashing it with
my thumb and then sliding the papery skin off. I'm making a pot
of black beans and we're standing beneath a poster of a hillside

covered with wildflowers over a Hopi saying, "Cover my earth mother, four times with many flowers." I'm nineteen and he's twenty-one and I'm on my way to Africa to see for myself what the hell I am.

But back in ninth grade we don't talk about any of that. One night when I'm alone and feeling bold I call Andre and invite him over to my house. When he gets there I pretend to be asleep, encouraging him with a sleepy wave to get into the bed with me, to lie with me so I won't feel so alone. After a few minutes we're kissing and then Andre is pushing against me, his big feet slipping in between the brass bars at the foot of my bed. We try to have sex but we're both clumsy, awkward, unsure. I imagine he's done it zillions of times and our inability to do it must be my fault. When it becomes clear that I'm way too nervous for his penis to get inside my tight-as-a-drum vagina, we're both embarrassed. He dresses, jumping into his tight 501s. Before he leaves he kisses me on the forehead, and then I listen to him go down the stairs and out the downstairs door of our building, which closes with a shudder and then a click.

The first time I go to Jesse's house I'm holding hands with his roommate, Len Black. Len opens the latch on the wooden gate at the end of the driveway and leads me back past some potted trees to the little door of Jesse's downstairs apartment. Inside it smells like a mixture of animals and cigarette smoke, with some sweet sticky menthol smell in the air that I can't place. Right away I love Jesse's apartment. It's small, only two rooms, a bathroom and a tiny kitchen, but on one wall of the living room there's a giant Keith Haring painting of a pregnant woman, her purple body surrounded by emphatic lines of red and yellow, and on another there's an old black-and-white photograph of a woman in a leotard standing in front of an elephant with her arms outstretched. Above the bed that's a sofa during the day, there's a color photograph of Nastassja Kinski wrapped up in a snake.

Jesse is a white boy who talks and acts black. He tucks button-down shirts into straight-legged pants to work at the law firm he answers phones for, and wears leather pants and snakeskin shoes at night, when he goes to house parties and clubs and drinks sweet black-people drinks like Malibu and pineapple and strawberry daiquiris. He's got curly light brown hair that's either wet-curled with curl activator or halfway to dreadlocks. He's got piercing green eyes and full pink lips, and when he opens his mouth he doesn't sound anything like I expect him to.

"Nah, cuz," he's saying to Len, who wants to borrow twenty dollars. "You still haven't even paid me back the money you owe me for the rent, how am I gonna lend you more money?" And when Tony starts talking about some boy up at school who took his money for a gram of weed and then never produced, Jesse starts in on him. "That nigga ain't shit, Tone, I told you not to be messin with him, didn't I? If you needed something you shoulda come to me, I woulda hooked you up."

Jesse sells everybody I know their weed, and can get his hands on anything else you might want: mushrooms, cocaine, and later on, when I'm in eleventh and twelfth grade, ecstasy. He's also an animal freak. The other room in his tiny apartment is filled with animals, and even though they smell up the entire place and he's always moaning about having to clean his animal room or having to spend this many dollars on a new cage or on live mice for Honey the snake's dinner, he loves his animals more than anything. He's got a ten-foot python, two iguanas, three lizards, a tarantula, and a box turtle. And there's always a cat or two moving in and out of Jesse's house too, winding its way around your legs as you sit at the tiny kitchen table, puffing on an indika joint and watching Jesse stir a pot of pasta sauce.

At first I go over to Jesse's only with Len, who lives there because he had to leave his own house for some reason I can't wholly discern because everybody gives me a different story. Either his fa-

ther drinks and beats him or his sister is being abused by both parents and they kicked him out when he stood up for her and raised
his fist at his father. I never get to the truth behind the rumors.

We end up there after going to the Saturday-afternoon scary
movie, *Poltergeist* or *Friday the Thirteenth Part Six*; or after school
we ride the bus there together, me avoiding going home to my
empty house. But after I stop seeing Len, after he scares me one
day by getting mad at me for giving another guy my phone number, and he shows me just how broken and violent and incoherent
he really is, I start going to Jesse's by myself when I know Len
won't be there, and leaving just before Jesse thinks he might be
home.

Those times I knock on the window carrying a big bag of junk
food, abstaining until I can crack it open in Jesse's toasty living
room. Three Musketeers, Snickers, barbecue and sour-cream-and-
onion potato chips, green-apple Jolly Ranchers. On nights my
mother is out of town this might be dinner if Jesse doesn't feed me
some real food. I gnaw through my stash as Sade sings "Smooth
Operator" or "Hang On to Your Love," and Jesse rolls a joint on
the inside of a top of an old shoe box. We talk about traveling to
Mexico, where a friend of his lives, and Singapore and Sri Lanka,
where he is dying to go. We talk about how fucked up Len is, and
about Michael and what it used to be like when they all, Tony,
Andre, Len, Jesse, Michael, and a bunch of other names with faces
I haven't seen, went to Washington, back in the day. There were
picnics organized by the girlfriends, trips to Six Flags, the prom.

We also, even though I don't really want to, talk about New
York. Jesse has never been and wants to know what it's like. I am
too embarrassed to mention Larchmont, and instead keep my talk

to the city and my references gritty, closer to the Bronx. He tells me he wants a big brass name belt and he wants to know, like all the other kids I meet in San Francisco, if a person can walk down a New York street without getting mugged. He wants to know what kind of weed you can get and if it's true that the dealers sell nickel and dime bags through bulletproof doors with slots that open only to accept money and push out weed. Is Thai stick or sensimilla more popular?

But he also wants to know about the trains, the graffiti artists, and the clubs he has heard about like Area and Studio 54, places I have never been. He's friends with a performance artist named Rhodessa Jones and he asks if I've ever heard of her brother, Bill T., a dancer and choreographer who has performed in New York with his lover and partner, Arnie Zane. Do I like Keith Haring, he wants to know, or Richard Avedon?

Jesse is the first person I know well who is like me: a border crosser, a human bridge. Downstairs in his two rooms he's surrounded by black people who jokingly make fun of him for being the blackest white boy on the planet, and upstairs he's surrounded by his white family, who love him to death even when they can't quite figure out what he's doing with his life and why he talks the way he does. What I'm attracted to is the way Jesse seems to do all of this moving up and down and in and out so seamlessly.

When I go upstairs one night to have dinner with his polite, slightly stiff, and decidedly upper-class parents, I wait to see if he will tone down his talk, if he will move his hands and face and body more like the white son I'm sure his parents want. When he doesn't and when I see his parents respond without hesitation or judgment, I am shocked at first, looking for some sign of parental denial or neglect, but they are attentive, caring, present. After that, Jesse becomes my hero.

Jesse doesn't tell me he's gay until I'm almost through high school. I've always suspected but still it's a bit of a shock. I'm happy for him, Tony and Len are cool and indifferent, but Michael says he can't believe his friend is a fag. He stops talking to Jesse then, right around the time he has a red, black, and green map of Africa tattooed on his left shoulder. For a few weeks Michael says he doesn't want me going to see Jesse, thinking I can shut down our friendship like I try to years later, when I am in college and I tell Jesse I won't see him unless he stops doing the drugs that I think are killing him, the crack and the speed that make him jittery all the time and keep him hollow, self-deflecting, locked into a job he hates and talking all the time about all the businesses he wants to start: a jewelry store, a pet shop, a catering company. It's not until then, my junior year in college, that I see how lonely Jesse is, how like me he is torn, ripped apart by belonging to two worlds and none at the same time.

E ven though we break up every other week and while we're broken up I go out with boys who could be considered Michael's friends, Michael and I are a big item, a serious couple. Even though we didn't keep in close touch while I was in New York, a letter here, a phone call there, the second I get back to San Francisco, I call him and he rides his ten-speed over to the square to meet me. After a few weeks Michael and I are together all the time, and when we're not together we're on the phone.

On the mornings that Michael has his mother's car, he drives me to school, stopping first at the McDonald's on Van Ness for a Sausage and Egg McMuffin. On the weekends he drives me to my job at Ivory, the hair salon my mother goes to on California Street. After I spend the day sweeping hair, making appointments, and being doted on by Ivory, Giovanni, Robert, and all the other gay men who go in and out of the shop, Michael comes to get me, waiting out front in his chugging car, staring anxiously through the front glass window, and beckoning me to hurry up.

When my mother is away, Michael spends the night and we try out every sexual position we can think of. We suck and lick and taste every single part of each other and then we shower, or we order pizza and eat it in front of the TV, his hand reaching over every few minutes to touch my young nipple. If my mother is home and his is too, we sneak into his basement, a dark room with no heat that his older brothers have renovated to look like the Parliament Funkadelic Mothership by covering all the walls with tinfoil and screwing purple tube lights in all the sockets. There's a couch that smells like mildew and sweat underneath torn plastic seat covers against one wall, and a black bar with a turntable on top against another. We lug a four-pack of wine coolers down there and drink them slow, talking and laughing and making out real quiet so his mother upstairs won't hear, so his sister and brother won't come in and embarrass us.

Michael's older brothers are already married and out of the house, but two of his siblings still live at home and torment him on a regular basis: his sister, who is always asking for money, and his brother, who is hostile, jabbing his fingers into Michael's chest and calling him names like punk and faggot whenever he passes. His mother works long hours as a nurse at San Francisco General, and Michael's father, or at least the man he thinks is his father until one day his mother tells him that in fact his father was somebody else, is dead.

After we have been going out for a few months, Michael spends more and more time taking care of one of his sister's children, the sweet, curious little girl she can't take care of herself. Instead of seeing him every day, I see him when he's not watching her, or driving his mother to work, or at his own job at the senior citizens' home across the street from our housing development, where I sometimes walk at five-thirty to pick him up.

If I get to the home early I go inside and watch Michael move around the tables in the fake-wood-paneled dining room, wheeling a cart and picking up dirty dishes behind gray-haired white women and men who barely notice he is there. Michael's is the only dark face in the room, all the others are back in the kitchen, where I sometimes go to wait for him and where the guys sometimes tell me I'm cute or that Michael is lucky to have a good girl like me, one that will come and wait for him.

After Michael has collected all the plates, scraped all the dishes, rewrapped the condiments, and stripped and sorted the tablecloths, he changes out of his uniform into his regular clothes and my Michael comes back to me again, even though I can still smell a mixture of grease, cooking food, and dishwashing cleaner in his hair, all around his collar, and on his hands.

Before we go home to my house to scrub him clean, we might take a walk around the fountains at the center of the upscale housing development across the street from my decidedly working-class one. Breathing in the smell of the pine trees all around and soothed by the sound of the water running through the fountains, Michael and I do a lot of our talking here. This is where he tells me that his mother lied to him about who his father was. This is where he tells me that he lost one job and has to go find another. This is where I tell him that my period is late, that I think I'm pregnant. It's where I tell him that I'm going to have an abortion, that it's going to happen at the French Medical Building on Geary and he better come.

When I tell my mother I am pregnant I am calm, sad, and tearful maybe, but not because I expect she's going to be mad. I walk into her bedroom after she's been meditating and the air around her is all quiet and still and stand beside her, next to her big wooden bed. When I tell her, Mom, I think I am pregnant, she responds without too long a hesitation. Find a doctor to get a test, she says. Once you know for sure, we'll schedule an abortion. She doesn't lecture me, she doesn't say, How did this happen, aren't you using birth control, she doesn't say much of anything except to call her boyfriend a few hours later and tell him. I hear her telling him over the bright yellow rotary phone in her study that I'm pregnant, that I've just told her this, and that she's exhausted. I hear her sighing as she speaks, the same sigh I hear when she worries about money, when she's feeling overwhelmed and retreats to her bedroom for hours, sometimes days.

The abortion happens on an overcast, rainy Friday afternoon. Michael has taken off from work and the three of them, Michael, my mother's boyfriend, Robert, and my mother, settle into the waiting area as a nurse takes me into a little room and tells me to take my clothes off and put my legs up into the stirrups. When I am lying there, naked and cold, with my legs splayed, I think about a girl I knew at Hommocks who got pregnant, and wonder if it was the same for her when she had her abortion. And I wonder if the stern, laconic doctor I met with the week before has plans to sterilize me. I wonder if she has thought it all out, how there shouldn't be any more black babies, and how sterilizing as many black women as she can will be doing her part for the cause.

When she finally comes in, my doctor, a short older white woman with gray hair, she doesn't look at me really, just tells me to get ready and then inserts a huge needle into my vagina. I feel a shot into what can only be my cervix and then I feel nothing. I hear the sound of the machine, a whirring, and I hear the nurse say certain things and I feel the two of them distinctly as they move in and out from between my legs. And then it is over and the doctor is telling me that I may bleed but not too much and if it doesn't stop by Monday I should call and come in again because that means there is an infection or some other problem.

My mother is the first one up when I come out from behind the little door, and Michael too is up, attentive, wanting to know how I feel, how was it, am I okay. Even though I'm a little shaky and it's not quite like nothing has happened, it's pretty close. I'm fine. I don't have cramps, I'm not bleeding, I'm not tired. When my mother asks me what I want to do, I say, Go to the movies! And so we go, ending up out at the Serramonte Center, watching a matinee of *Purple Rain*. The fact that Prince's mother is white and his father is black doesn't register, I'm too caught up in the sexiness of the music, the images of Prince riding Appolonia on his motorcycle down at the reservoir, and how fucked up it is when Morris Day and his boys throw two women into a dumpster. Afterward, we drive down to Fisherman's Wharf and pick up a couple of cracked crabs and a loaf of sourdough bread for dinner, and we go home to our little apartment and eat, listening to a new Chuck Mangione record Robert brought over.

I don't really think about the abortion again, except to stop Michael from trying to have sex too soon afterward, and to dream for a few seconds here and there about what a baby belonging to me and Michael would look like. I know that my mother had an abortion before they were legal and so I know to be grateful that I didn't have to have a baby way before I was old enough to take care of it, but other than all of that stuff, the baby doesn't cross my mind. I don't feel guilt, like my roommate in college says I should years later, and I don't feel sad the way pamphlets on abortion say I might.

It seems eerie to me only later on, the way the whole thing goes by without me having any strong feelings about it, no ritual of mourning, not one serious thought about ending something that could have been. I'm twenty-eight and co-parenting my partner's biological child. He's eight years old and looking up at me and I swear I see his mother's face and that's when I wonder what my baby would have been like. Does she remember in her cellular memory being ripped from my womb?

A few nights after we see *Purple Rain* my mother comes into my room and lies down on my bed while I finish up some homework and get my clothes ready for school the next day. As I lay my outfit out on the chair by the window, we talk. She wants to know where Michael and I hang out on the weekends when I'm not at work, and I tell her about the parking attendant booth in Japantown that some of his friends work at, the way we all meet up there and talk shit, the girls sticking close to the little metal box with windows while the boys toss a football up and down the length of the parking lot. She nods skeptically and then I turn to her and out of the blue tell her that I'm not learning anything at Washington, and that if I stay there through twelfth grade I'll know less than when I started. I tell her that I need to go to a private school.

I don't know where this comes from, really, this sudden excla-
mation, because it's not like I've been thinking about it and it's
not like I know anybody my age who is actually in a private
school. But I have just had an abortion at fourteen, and we don't
read books in my English class, only endless mimeographed hand-
outs, and Michael's friends in college work for minimum wage
parking cars.

My mother, thank God, doesn't hestitate. Lifting herself off
the bed, she pats my arm and says, "Okay, we'll look."

the mushy part of Rebecca the mushy par

I have never been at home in my body. Not in its color, not in its size or shape. Not in its strange, unique conglomeration of organic forms and wavy lines. In the mirror, I am always too pale, too pasty, not honey-colored, not the glamorous-sounding café au lait. My breasts are always too small, my thighs too fat, my gait inelegant, my neck too long. There is an awkwardness to my body, a lack of grace, as if the racial mix, the two sides coming together in my body, have yet to reconcile.

Thank God I have, as my friends of color call it, rhythm. For black folks, "having rhythm" is like speaking a different language, and pity you if you don't know the words. "Poor thing," I myself have snickered about a mixed person with no groove, clinging to a rare, luxurious feeling of inclusion, "the mix just didn't turn out right."

But I can dance, my body can find a beat and hold it, my hips, my pelvis can find the bass, can find the drum. My black friends and lovers tell me this is one of my redeeming qualities, this ability to move, to embody the music. "Your mama kicked in there, boy," a girlfriend will say. Or a lover, "That's when I know you're black, when you start moving those hips." And then she'll put one hand in the small space between my waist and hip and follow me as I move, her eyes drunkenly watching as I throw my head back.

And it's true, even though I remember dancing with my father to Roberta Flack and Al Green; he danced a soulful version of the hustle, not the bump. And it's my mama who danced all night to Bob Marley, who twirled around the kitchen grilling lamb chops and singing along with Stevie Wonder. But where does that leave me? Ashamed of one half, grateful for the other? Ashamed one moment, proud the next, my comfort determined solely by context?

When I am under Michael in the dark, when I have my head under the covers and am sucking Luca's smooth, white penis, when Andre is stretching his hard, muscle-bound body over me as the fog seeps in the window above my head, when Ray Martinez grabs the back of my neck in the movie theater and pushes his tongue farther into my mouth, I feel all my fear and anxiety about being liked, fitting in, knowing where and who I am melt away. I feel I am finally just the soft part of who I am, the mushy part of Rebecca, the part underneath the hard outer layer whose face frowns and shoulders tense, who watches every move to know how to follow. Their attention is the salve that coats the wound, is the sound that drowns out all the people who don't like black white girls, who don't like white black girls, who don't like me, the skin on my body having determined this long before I have even had a chance to speak.

untasted flavor of the month an untasted flavor of the

W hen we arrive for the second day of the application
process at Urban, the small, hippie private school my mother and
I choose over its stuffy, more collegiate rival, we are shown to a
small back room in an old Victorian row house. It is warm and
comfortable, with a squarish blue sofa and soft, intimate lighting.
A door at the back opens onto an outdoor area where students sit
casually, eating lunch from crinkled brown paper bags. Here at
Urban students call teachers by their first names, and even though
I assume that most of the kids are rich, they don't look it to me.
Instead of the fancy, expensive clothes and perfectly styled hair I
expect, most of them look like they just woke up, threw on a
sweatshirt, and rode their skateboards to school.

Yesterday I counted two black students out of fifty, and today
I haven't seen one yet, but I like Urban anyway. I like the way two
students, a boy and girl, run the first part of the application
process, giving me materials to fill out and then interviewing me
to see if they think I'll be a good addition to their school. I like the
way the actual classroom building, next door to the office build-

ing I'm in now, has a big skylight in the center and a huge sculpture made of branches hanging down from it. I like that the classes are small, the reading lists full of books I want to read, and that as I walk around several people ask if they can help me find what I'm looking for. When I sit in on a teacher named Joanna's Latin American Lit class, I know that Urban is the place for me.

Joanna is tall and striking and tells me after class that she comes from Catalonia, northern Spain. She speaks Spanish and English with a lisp and wears tall brown leather boots and a skirt covered with bright, flowery embroidery. Her shiny black hair is cut in a severe bob that accentuates her prominent nose and deep-set dark brown eyes. Joanna has her students reading *One Hundred Years of Solitude,* and when I visit her class, a tiny rectangle of a room with lots of dark wood and a wall of windows facing onto the street, she reads aloud from the book. Magically, I am transported to the world of Aurelianos and black and white daguerreotypes, of white and gold butterflies and burning night fevers that won't die.

When she puts her weathered copy of the book down and turns to the students for their response, her eyes are brimming with tears I am not sure the rest of the class notices but which stir something in me, some quiet affinity. The students talk at length about language and tone, about character and style, but I am more interested in Joanna and how she listens to each of them intently, how she makes little high-pitched clucking noises when one of them says something particularly astute. I feel something physically shift in my body as I imagine myself asking questions, contributing my thoughts.

But I am still only in the application process and even though the young woman who interviewed me told me I have a good chance and she thinks I would be a great Urban student, I still have not met with the headmaster, and even though I'm looking forward to the next Urban experience, I'm nervous too, wondering if he'll like me, if he'll think I'm Urban material. When he walks in I can tell it's him because he's the man in all the pictures around the office, framed color photos of the headmaster and his wife surrounded by kids at a private school up north he used to run.

He's wearing a button-down flannel shirt and jeans and carrying a mug of tea which seems tiny against his tall stocky frame. I can't help but think he looks like he should be chopping wood instead of running an institution, but that informality is what I like about Urban, so I take his outfit as a sign: The emphasis here is on what you say, not what you wear. And so I listen carefully for Carl's first words, for what he's going to say after he walks in and sits in the big chair behind the desk and looks reservedly over at my mother and me sitting together on the boxy blue sofa.

This is what he says, without a hello, an introduction, a hi nice to meet you I'm so-and-so and your name is . . . He leans back in his chair, peers at us from behind thick square glasses like the kind I had to wear in shop class one year, and says, straight out with no provocation of any kind: Well the first thing I must tell you folks is that there's just no financial aid available. Then he leans farther back in his chair and kicks his feet up onto the desk like an old James Dean.

For a split second I don't catch the assumption, don't see the train of thought he's following. I'm just stunned that he hasn't introduced himself, hasn't thrown out any icebreakers to make me feel more comfortable, hasn't said something about my test scores or my interview or what the next step in the application process is. But as my mother's hand tightens around mine, in the space of milliseconds I get it. We're black and so we must need financial aid.

By then my mother's body is stiff and her eyes icy and she's telling this white man coldly, in a way I can tell she's had to do many times before, that we didn't ask for any financial aid, and then we are up and out of the office and the headmaster is following us out and down the hall. Now seeing paying diversity rather than non-paying diversity, he tries to apologize, to stammer his way through something about a misunderstanding, but my mother and I are out of the building and I'm thinking about Joanna and the tears in her eyes and what it would be like if my big white father were here with us, and his white Volvo was parked outside. Would it be different then? And then I think about the student who interviewed me and how she said I'd be a good Urban student and then we're driving away from the wood-framed building that was almost mine, turning down Masonic after a huge orange 43 Masonic bus passes, on our way home.

Three weeks later, when the letter of acceptance comes in the mail, my mother tells me that she is too tired and too busy working on a screenplay to accompany me back to Urban to enroll. Without telling me beforehand, she hires someone to go back to the school with me to fill out all the paperwork, to act as a liaison between the school and my adults. I miss my mother walking up the speckled smooth cement stairs with me on the first days of school, but I am so excited about being an Urban student I don't dwell on it until the school has an open house for new students and their parents and my mother sends the woman she hired.

I get so angry at my mother for hiring someone to take care of me that I have a rare tantrum, complete with banging doors and cursing and telling my mother that I'll go by myself. In response she writes me a note on a card with a mother gorilla and her child on the front. Inside it says that she is sorry she didn't consult with me but she has just been so busy and so tired working. She writes that she is proud of me for being independent and able to deal so well without her. She writes that I will have to continue to do what I always say I can: take care of myself.

W hen the school year starts, Michael picks me up in the mornings like usual and drives me to school, except instead of driving out to the Avenues with the flat suburban-style houses and wide empty sidewalks, he drives me into the heart of the Haight, past the panhandle of Golden Gate Park and the stores with psychedelic Grateful Dead stickers and tie-dye shirts cluttering their front windows. I'm usually late, downing a cup of carrot or orange juice as I kiss Michael goodbye, slam the door of his car, and sprint up the carpeted stairs into school.

My first class in the morning is Introduction to Drawing and in it I'm the only sophomore circling the still life in the middle of the room. Suzi Khan, the girl I imagine to be the richest in the school because she drives a red 450SL Mercedes with her name on the license plate, is in my class, and so is Libby, her best friend, who is blond and has gigantic breasts, which I assume at least partly explains her popularity with all the senior boys. Even though I have no friends at school to tell me this, I know that Suzi got her car when she was sixteen and that her father is some kind of doctor. I know that Libby lives in Pacific Heights and has a boyfriend here at school that she's been going out with since sophomore year.

Other than these small tidbits, my classmates remain a mystery to me, and in between the hours that Michael drops me off and Tony picks me up, I am mostly alone, surrounded by one hundred or so laughing, skateboarding, coffee-drinking, Hacky

Sack–playing, U2 and UB40 listening-to white kids and six or seven wigged-out-looking, trying-to-be-cool-acting brown ones from San Francisco. At lunchtime, while my classmates sprawl out in the sun on the sidewalk across the street from school smoking cigarettes and eating pizza or smoothies from the health food store, I walk up Haight Street to the market a few blocks over, down closer to the park.

Every day I buy the same small items: a lemonade, a bag of chips, a bag of plum candies, and I ask the small Asian woman behind the counter for the same thing: a jack and avocado sandwich on whole wheat bread with tomato, mayonnaise, and mustard. From my side of the cash register, I peer over the countertop scale and shift my body to let customers pass, watching as this now familiar woman cuts and slices and puts together my sandwich. I laugh as her baby daughter of three or four clutches at and plays around her knees. We don't talk much, but I am grateful for her daily presence, her careful preparation of my food, the way she parents me without knowing.

I am also grateful for Richard. Richard, who teaches algebra and looks like a movie star, who rides to school on a motorcycle, wearing corduroys, Birkenstocks with socks, and a beat-up leather jacket, his dirty-blond hair sticking out the edges of his busted-up black helmet. All the girls have crushes on Richard, but when pressed, he talks about his wife and constantly fiddles with the gold band around his ring finger.

We don't think that to him we must look like toddlers; we, all of us, myself included, think we can seduce Richard, that when he leans down over one of us to explain why x goes over to the other side when you work the equation, his eyes and nostrils practically humming with intensity, that really he likes us especially, that we are the one girl in the whole school who could pull it off, who could make Richard love a high school girl.

But really Richard is too busy trying to convince girls that they can do math, that it's easier, really, to figure it out than it is to look away and pretend to know, certainly easier than it is to get the teacher to fall in love with you. In my first days in Richard's class I tell him, when he comes around to my seat at the big table we use as a desk, that my father always said I won't be good at math because my mother isn't. Richard looks at me, blinking his big brown eyes as if he hasn't heard anything I've said. Then he tells me that of course I can do math. It's not that hard, Richard says in my afternoon Algebra Two class, all I have to do is think and not run, think and not run, think and not run until I work out the problem.

And there is Bill. Bill is big and burly with greasy dark hair and a sly smile that shows coffee- and nicotine-stained teeth. He teaches The Greeks, and even though he says I'm one of his favorite students, he still admonishes me harshly on my evaluation, the grade-free handwritten report we get instead of a traditional report card. Be on time! Write clearer, less vague sentences! Give more examples! Bill corrects my papers, painstakingly typed out on my mother's new electric typewriter, with a fat red pen. I am obsessed with Iphigenia, the way she feels as she is being marched to her death by her entire community, her mother and sisters walking her stoically to the cliff. But Bill wants less editorial, more exposition!

Folding his stubby fingers at his belly and looking at me skeptically as I try to wriggle out of a criticism, Bill pushes me to think, not just to feel. He wants me to engage the text, to analyze the writing, to decode the message. He thinks my outrage has a place, but not until I've let the material speak to me in other ways. Bill tells me that I'm gifted but that I cannot coast, I must work hard. For Bill's class I do my first series of drafts, crossing out words and replacing them, changing sentences around, rephrasing thoughts. Doing the rewrites wounds my naive pride and I hate it, but when I'm done I feel a tremendous sense of accomplishment, handing Bill my sheaf of crisp, white papers.

And Debra too, who teaches Introduction to Photography. Even though she's too harried to mentor me, she hands me a camera and some film and tells me to go look, to see how my world looks inside of a rectangular frame. I take pictures that aren't very good of everything: staircases, trees, bus windows, punks with bright orange mohawks sitting on the ground in front of Double Rainbow, the Haight ice cream shop. The camera around my neck allows me to talk to people I ordinarily wouldn't, like Giovanni Del Rosso, this beautiful Italian boy from Venezia who follows me off a bus one day when I'm taking pictures, telling me in Italian that I'm *bellissima*.

Giovanni becomes my friend, taking me to seafood dinners on Polk Street and feeding me mussels, clams, linguine. *"Frutti di mare!"* he yells, holding a clam to my mouth in one hand, a glass of white wine in the other. "Eat! Eat!" We walk up the hills of North Beach together on foggy San Francisco nights holding hands as he describes Venice, the endless water, how lonely he is there with his family who only want him to marry and join the Del Rosso export business. In the darkroom I find pictures of Giovanni's hands, the prominent collarbone at the base of his neck, his high cheekbones and nose in profile. I like being in the darkroom with pieces of him, sliding the squares of paper around in the magic liquid. I like watching the timer, examining my out-stretched hand in the soft red light. I like hearing the thumping of the other students as they walk across the floor above my head.

On weekends when I'm not doing some of the mass quantities of homework Joanna assigns, like translating pages of *One Hundred Years of Solitude* from Spanish to English, I hang out with Michael. Sometimes I ride with him to drop his mother off at work, and one night I ride with him to visit one of his friends who happens to sell cocaine. I go along with Michael's charade of total cool in front of the tall light-skinned dealer, crossing my legs coyly and dabbing my pinkie finger in the pile of coke to rub the stuff against my gums for a freeze.

I have been with Michael for so long, I trust him. It doesn't occur to me that he would do anything to hurt me. Except that late one night he shows up at my door crying because he's slept with another girl and he feels ashamed and sorry and says he'll never do it again. Except that he starts to call me half breed now that I go to Urban, half breed because he says my white comes out when I'm at Urban, when I slip and say *like* every other word or when I ask him if he's heard the new Police record, or if I analyze a movie for too long or with too much intensity. He tells me I sound like a white girl. He tells me that he forgets sometimes that I'm not a real sister. He says this like he's joking, with a big bright white smile, but I don't hear it as a joke.

I hear it as territory I'm supposed to defend.

B ut white guys do start to factor big in my life. There's Giovanni, whom I let kiss me in my room in front of my purple and green Monet waterlily posters, and there's Tad, a tall lanky punk rock boy, and there's Rob, this bartender I start to date when I'm in New York for Project Month, Urban's version of a work/study program in which we all go somewhere for a month to live and learn. I apply to work as an intern at the Museum of Modern Art, where except for me and the guards, everyone is white, educated, moneyed, shaking my hand to learn my pedigree, and then dismissing me if it fails to impress.

Even still, I love the museum: the strong vertical lines and luxe interior, the naked voluptuous woman in the sculpture garden. I spend my days cataloging slides and talking to young children about the Miró and Picasso paintings on the pristine white walls, and fume privately about the absence of works by artists of color. One day when I am feeling particularly bold, I stride up to the president of the museum, a tall, dour, intimidating man in his sixties, and demand to know why the one painting on display by an

African-American painter is hung on a fire-exit door behind the escalator. He looks at me blankly before saying that he hasn't any idea.

At night in New York I dance on tables at the Pyramid Club and Area if I can get in, and I hang out with my über-cool boss, Philip Yenawine, who in a few years will create a Day Without Art to commemorate those dead or dying from AIDS. With Philip I go to cavernous lofts in SoHo with hi-tech eighties track lighting, granite kitchen countertops, and blue and red neon accents. I spot David Byrne, Keith Haring, Malcolm McLaren, and Lauren Hutton; I drink red wine and feel like the coolest girl in the world.

But when Philip's son Tad and I fool around the day after a party like this, sitting on one of the plush projector-room sofas in the museum where Tad's supposed to be doing God knows what and I'm supposed to be delivering a box of old movie posters, this total white boy takes his hand from under my shirt to stroke my curly hair and ask me out to dinner and it occurs to me that my blackness means something different in the downtown New York scene. My blackness is cool in a way it wasn't at Hommocks, in a way it wasn't at Washington. It's something that makes me hot, special, attractive, an untasted flavor of the month.

From New York I write Michael postcards that I buy in the museum shop. I write to him about New York, which he's never seen, on the backs of paintings and photographs by Georgia O'Keeffe, Jackson Pollock, and Henri Cartier-Bresson. I write about the subway and the parties and I write about the music on the street and on the radio, music that hasn't reached the West

Coast yet, like Lisa Lisa's "I Wonder If I Take You Home," which plays on 98.7 KISS FM, like, every five minutes.

I tell him I miss him, which I do, but I don't tell him about Tad or Philip and his boyfriend, and I don't tell him about the museum, about all the things I'm learning about art, about the Guerrilla Girls show that I go to where all the artists wear gorilla masks on their faces to protest gender discrimination in the art world, about this black artist named Jean-Michel Basquiat who is crossing over from graffiti to high art. I don't tell Michael about all the things that might mark me more in his eyes as the half-breed race traitor I feel I am becoming. I certainly don't tell him that in New York, all my friends are white.

When I return to Urban I am changed, more independent, more cosmopolitan. I still love Michael, but I never see Maya or Tony anymore. By now I am well trained in not breaking the code, not saying something too white around black people, or too black around whites. It's easier to be quiet, aloof, removed than it is to slip and be made fun of for liking the wrong thing, talking the wrong way, being the wrong person, the half-breed oreo freak. At the booth, being unable to integrate my experiences into one relatively cohesive self that is flexible and unstudied and relaxed means that I am stiff and strained, nervous and sweating when I should be able to laugh, play video games, and catch the football the fellas sometimes jokingly throw my way.

Instead of *intimidating,* the word white people have used to describe what they find unsettling about me, Michael says I am *snobby,* the term black people use. He tells me that people, our friends, say I think I'm better than everybody else, that I know more than everybody else. The only people I feel comfortable with are my teachers. Richard, Bill, Joanna, Debra. They grant me the exquisite luxury of feeling normal by focusing not on my skin but on my mind, my curiosity, my writing skills.

When I am fifteen, my teachers save my life.

MONROE

The first full sentence I say to Andrew after we meet and work together for a few days is, "Hold this, I'm bleeding like a sow." I have my period and I need him to hold the heavy walkie-talkie I rip out of the holster at my waist. He's a white boy in faded jeans and a soft old white tee shirt, a pack of Marlboro lights jammed in his back pocket, and I'm a caramel-colored girl with curly out-of-control near to dreadlocked hair, wearing striped purple pants and yellow high-top Reeboks. He's the head set-production assistant on the movie I'm working on, the movie my mother has been so busy writing the screenplay for, based on one of her books, and I'm the first p.a. under him.

It's my first real job and so I hustle when he or any one of my other superiors asks me to do something. I run when the director says he needs something right away, and yell when I need some-body in a big truck to turn his engine off because we're rolling. When I ask Andrew to hold my walkie-talkie I've just come from B camera down the hill, half running all the way up to the honey wagons, super conscious that I've been told to come right back.

He is signing out a couple of actors, holding the sheet down on a metal clipboard as they slide a pen over the paper. When I come out of the tiny Formica john a few minutes later, he's alone, sitting on the steps and smoking a cigarette.

As I step down and cross in front of him, he doesn't say a lot to me, just makes a sarcastic joke: Do you say that to everybody you want to do you a favor? He takes a hard drag from his cigarette, shrugs his shoulders, says Jesus as he tosses off a half laugh and rolls his eyes down to the ground. I'm fully prepared to write him off, to say, Whatever, dude, to his attitude and throw it back at him, but I don't. He seems so vulnerable sitting there, looking tough and lonely in his white-boy silence.

I sit down next to him, ask him where he's from, how long he's worked for the director. I can tell he's surprised I'm talking to him, looking him in the eye, trying to find out who he is. I've watched how most of the crew treat Andrew, how he blends in, fades away. How he handles this by being even more serious about his job, and keeping to himself. I know this feeling, and that knowing compels me to penetrate the wall he's built around himself.

I ask about his parents, especially his mother, since everybody has that on me, they know all about my mother while I know nothing of theirs. She's a writer, he says, screenplays, teleplays. My father is a record producer from the sixties, he says. You know the Who, the Kinks? I say his last name out loud, making it a question. Yeah, he's Jewish, Andrew says, I'm half Jewish. Me too, I say. And then we are talking about what is going on at B camera and how real the fake snow we are filming looks. By the time I am called to accompany an actor to the set, something has happened between Andrew and me, something has started.

. . .

W eeks go by. At the end of fourteen-hour days we all ride in the crew bus back to the Holiday Inn. Me, Andrew, Bruce the DGA trainee, Vicki the second AD and the gaffer, electricians, and grips. I ride with Todd, a beefy, fine, six-foot-five electrician with full lips and kinky brown hair, in the back, and Andrew sits, his wavy hair lightening every day in the sun, way up front, alone or with one of the best boys. Even though Andrew and I are close all day, when it's time to make public my allegiance I go to the back of the bus with Todd rather than take a seat next to Andrew. Once we step off the bus, though, it's Andrew and I who walk together with our arms touching past the mini pool at the center of the hotel, Andrew and I who ask one of the drivers if they can take us to Kmart after we shower so that we can buy some tapes and whatever else we can find to spend our per diem on.

And it's Andrew and I who lie in my room together with the air conditioner on high later, listening to Sting sing "Set Them Free" and making out, eating fried catfish from the fish joint up the road and drinking ice cold beer.

A fter six weeks of working our asses off in the hot North Carolina sun, Andrew and I are pretty sure we're in love. I cannot imagine living without his constant, generous adoration, the way he looks over my body again and again, finding and appreciating each beauty mark, every sloping curve. I thrill watching him saunter down the aisle at the Waffle House in his cowboy boots, faded Levi's, and worn button-down shirt. I get off on the fact that

I know from experience what his ass looks like underneath his jeans, how long and how smooth his dick is, how fleshy and pink his big-for-a-white-boy lips are. I like that I have come to know the odor emanating from his thighs, that I have begun to think of him and his body as my very own to taste and feel and savor.

And I like that Andrew comes from a world I don't know but to which I find myself undeniably attracted. At dinner he talks about directors I've never heard of: Robert Altman, John Schlesinger, John Cassavetes, throwing their names around like they're old friends. When we go to the movies he stays until the very end, studying the credits, tracking friends and acquaintances, applauding their work. He notices a film director's style, the way s/he uses the camera, the performances s/he draws out of the cast, the choice of film stock.

I'm so drunk with new ideas and fantastic sex that I don't see the problems. Like the fact that I'm only fifteen and Andrew is twenty-one. Like the fact that Andrew thinks I'm seventeen. Like the fact that even though I want to know what Influence Gena Rowlands is Under, staring out from a Cassavetes film poster in his bathroom, I don't ask Andrew to rent the film or even what it is about because I feel I have to pretend to know certain things in order to blend in enough to become one of his world. Like the fact that race, my blackness and his whiteness in particular, while not yet a problem for us, is clearly a problem for everybody else.

One night after we save three weeks of per diem and decide to spend it on a trip to New York after the movie wraps, Andrew calls his father, the blind record producer in Los Angeles, to tell him he's found the girl he wants to marry. His father wants to know more, and I listen, pretending not to as Andrew describes me: my intelligence, my attractiveness, my race. The next morning his father calls back in rage. He had a nightmare. Something he can't altogether remember but which featured Andrew lying in bed with his black girlfriend and a group of Klansmen coming after him with a rope. His father is convinced it is some kind of warning. Here is what he wants to know: Why on earth is Andrew dating a nigger?

A fter the movie wraps, Andrew and I head first to San Francisco, where he waits outside in my mother's car while I run into Michael's house to break up with him. Once I'm inside, looking into his face and surrounded by his books and bedcovers and all of his mother's slipcovered furniture, a part of me wants to stay. To tell Andrew I have made a mistake and he should go home. And yet another part, the part that wins, is cold, shut down, closing a chapter the way I have closed so many. I focus on Andrew waiting in the car, and don't allow myself the feelings settling in my stomach. I say things in a patronizing tone, like, Well, it had to happen sometime, and This just won't work.

With one hand I touch Michael's head. It's over, I say melodramatically, the way I've seen in the movies. I'm seeing someone else. Stunned, Michael looks down, shakes his head. And then, collecting himself, he is angry, demanding to know who I have been seeing and have we slept together and how long has it been going on. I take a breath and tell him. Instantly he's on his feet, gesturing angrily with his hands. I notice that the muscles in his calves and thighs are rock hard and bulging as he stands. Oh, come on, Rebecca, he shouts, his face contorted and indignant. It's bad enough you slept with someone else, but a white boy? And then he's almost laughing. You're leaving me for a *white* boy?

LOS ANGELES

When Andrew takes me to the house his mother is staying in on Palm Drive in Santa Monica, my hair is curly and free and I put my best earrings, purple titanium rectangles with little diamond studs at one end, on in the car as we fly down the 10 freeway in Andrew's black convertible Mustang. L.A. is hot and dusty and dry, and we are here to get a few things from Andrew's Tarzana apartment before we go to New York.

Andrew's apartment is three white boxes held together with dirty beige carpet, but I love it. In the mornings Andrew wakes me up with his camera in my face and then documents me until we leave the house; as I brush my teeth and wash my face, as I take my orange tank top off and step into the shower, as I sit reading in the big armchair in his living room. As he snaps, Andrew tells me over and over again that I am beautiful. Look at the light on you there, look at your eyes, your hair, the way you drink water from a glass! As he moves around me I feel a strange self-consciousness, that I am being looked at, that I am the object—

finally—of someone's attention, curiosity, love. It is something I do not know yet how to let in, to integrate. And yet I do, staring back at Andrew on the other side of the lens and allowing myself to be admired, to become the woman he sees.

In the afternoons we go to the movies or to the Ralph's grocery store to buy food to cook in his little apartment. We buy tortillas for burritos, tomatoes, jack cheese, and big jugs of drinking water. We buy six-packs of cold Corona. It's so hot we run from air conditioner to air conditioner, from store to store, and keep the windows of the Mustang rolled all the way down. Which is how they are as we drive to Palm Drive, all fresh from making love and showering, cooking together and eating. Andrew's mother is renting a wooden bungalow that sits behind two enormous palm trees, their thick trunks dominating the grassy front yard.

The first thing his mother does is offer us a drink, and then she's giving Andrew the latest draft of her script to read and asking him to take a look at something wrong with the plumbing, and then she's telling me and him that I'm darling, that we're a darling couple. And then she's asking if he's told his father yet about me and Andrew tells her about the dream and they both call him an asshole. As they talk I remember the day before, when we went to Andrew's father's house in Studio City and went swimming in his pool, listening to an advance copy of a Peter Gabriel album Andrew found on the turntable behind the bar.

Andrew jackknifed into the water as "Sledgehammer" blared through the sliding glass doors—*this will be my testimony sledge I'll be your sledgehammer*—and I sat tentatively on a deck chair in the hot, hazy L.A. sun, feigning relaxation and wondering what would happen if his father happened to come home and find us there. Would he rerun the lynching scenario, would he tell me to get out? And then I wondered how much Andrew and his father had in common. Would Andrew ever turn on me? Would he ever look up one day and see not me but a nigger?

in the "real" world blood strikes back in the "real" world

BELLINGHAM

Come fall, Andrew and I are inseparable even though he lives in Los Angeles and I live in San Francisco. Every weekend I am on a plane or he is, spending up all the money we made over the summer and some that Andrew has been saving since he graduated from high school. We take red-eye flights that cost thirty-nine dollars each way. I learn to drive from our house to the San Francisco airport in thirteen minutes, and when he's late or I'm early I sit and write sketches about the people I see at the airport: the young Japanese couple nuzzling at the big open mouth of the plane, the elderly man hooked up to oxygen boarding in a wheelchair with an orange backpack on his lap, the husband with his briefcase kissing his anxious wife and dazed-looking kids goodbye. When I finally spot Andrew, I imagine what I would write about us if I was watching: the artsy-looking brown dreadlocked girl and the dorky pale white guy in the checkered jacket.

When we get back to my house, Andrew sleeps late or reads books about screenplay structure quietly on the sofa while I write papers on the hard beige Macintosh computer my father sent me for my sixteenth birthday, papers about Robespierre, about how God speaks to the Israelites in the Old Testament, the role of the media in the Vietnam War. When we go out walking or to play Frisbee in Golden Gate Park or when we are eating or lying still in bed, Andrew and I talk. We talk about my mother and his mother and how they both needed us to be grown-ups before we were grown. We talk about his mother's drinking, the departure of the stepfather he grew up calling Dad, the fights he had with his father, who all but abandoned him and his twin sister when they were children. And then we talk about what we want to be, what we dream for ourselves, what we want to make out of what we have.

I want to make films, write, and be a therapist, all arts that require observation, which is what I seem to do best, holding myself at a distance from whatever is going on. One day walking home from school, I watch as a man beats a woman on the street in broad daylight. When I try to stop him, he threatens to kill me. When I wait and offer to drive the woman home, she tells me that her man will be back for her, that the man who just beat her with a telephone receiver and left her bleeding on the sidewalk is her husband and he loves her.

When I reach my house I don't know what else to do but make my way to my desk. In twenty-five minutes I write my first real essay, a stream-of-consciousness piece on witnessing a woman being beaten on a street corner and my failed attempt to rescue her. I feel a strange solace when I put down the pen, a clean, quiet calm that feels better than anything else so far.

Andrew is a writer too. He leaves me notes under my pillow that I find days later when I'm changing the sheets. He writes me beautiful poems, words scrawled in blue ballpoint pen across a pad with his name printed across the top. I love everything Andrew writes, the way he doesn't hold back his feelings, the way he tells me a hundred different ways that our connection is profound.

At Thanksgiving, I go with Andrew to his mother's house in Bellingham, in Washington state, where he grew up. I meet his best friends from high school, Zack and John, whom I've heard so much about I can hardly believe they are actually standing in front of me: Zack the dumb stud with the huge penis, John the geeky, diffident pothead with a head full of blond curls, the three of them together with their Led Zeppelin concert jerseys and faded Levi's, the whitest, countryest boys I've ever met.

One night as we sit around eating turkey and stuffing leftovers, drinking beer and playing cards, Zack casually says something about some dumb nigger he saw or knew or had to deal with, I can't remember which, only that the words walked out of his mouth as easily as if he were saying good morning. And then Andrew says, Zack come on, man, and John shifts in his chair nervously, and Zack smiles stupidly at the big shit he's just taken in the middle of our party. From my seat at the table they become dumb rednecks, including the one I love, and a wave of nausea, which I try to suppress by opening and taking a swig of another beer, comes over me.

When it is clear that no one else is going to speak, I ask Zack if he often calls black people niggers and how he'd like to be called a piece of white trash. I ask if he's ever known any black people and whether he learned to call us niggers from his parents or his peers or both. I ask how it makes him feel to call someone by a name that belittles them. Does it make him feel bigger? What made him feel so small that he needs to feel that much bigger? Before I can catch myself I am yelling and Andrew is fidgeting in his chair and I am thinking, How in the hell we are going to make it through the night, let alone the rest of this holiday vacation?

A couple of hours later, when Zack and John are both drunk and stoned and heading loopily for their car, I ask, even though a part of me could care less, if they are sober enough to drive. Andrew puts a protective arm around me and tells me not to worry, the three of them on any given weekend in high school drove, and sometimes crashed, full of a lot more pot and alcohol than they've got in them now. I feel sick. This image of white boys out of control, drunk and hurling the word *nigger* around, frightens me, reminds me of lynching photographs I've seen. Looking into Andrew's smiling brown eyes I feel a deep uneasiness, like suddenly I'm separate from him and on the other side of a long, treacherous tunnel I'm not sure I'll be able to get through.

As the sun slowly rises through the blinds in what used to be his sister's bedroom, Andrew responds to my anger by trying to assure me that Zack really is the most harmless guy. He's the one who just talks shit to get a rise out of people, the one who is a little slow and would never hurt anyone intentionally. I stare in disbelief as Andrew spins a yarn about Zack coming through for him and understanding him when others didn't. Before he can finish I launch into a lecture on racism and how he needs to hold his friends accountable. If he really wants to make a difference, I say, he'll talk seriously to Zack and try to beat him into this century.

I'm yelling this at Andrew and it is what I mean, but under-neath, what I am also saying, in a tiny voice that doesn't come out, is that if you really want to be with me, if you really want to show me that you aren't a racist redneck white boy, you'll give some-thing up, you'll take a risk and show your friends, your family, your whomever that I mean more to you than their comfort. You will prove your humanity to me by loving me in the face of all this bullshit.

What Andrew does, after I finish my tirade and look over at him with tears streaming down my face, is put his arms around me and agree with everything I've said. He apologizes and says he has never had to think about this from any other perspective but his own and he sees how truly horrible it, meaning racism, is. He says he will talk to Zack, that Zack's and John's provincialism is one of the reasons he sees them only once a year. He assures me that he's not like they are and that he loves me and is grateful to me for teaching him more about the world and the people in it. And Andrew tells me later, much later after we have finally suc-cumbed to exhaustion and are tucked snugly beneath yellow cot-ton sheets and down comforters which protect us from the wicked chill outside our window, that he won't ever leave.

Twenty years after Mississippi, a small group of students stay on after one of my lectures about young women and men and feminism to ask me the personal, more intimate questions they do not feel comfortable raising in front of the larger, more contentious crowd. Of the ten or so who remain, six or seven look as if they are of mixed parentage, as if we could be in the same tribe.

After introducing herself, a young, pretty, dark-skinned woman asks how she should explain being "mixed" to her "half-white" and "half-black" daughter. "Tell her the plain truth," I say, trying not to to sound smug. And my words don't go over well. The young mother steps in a little closer, putting her hand on her hip before she speaks. "But the world will see her, treat her, as black. Why should I confuse the issue?" She fixes me with a stare. "I want to prepare her for the *real* world."

It is true that in the "real" world blood strikes back. For marrying a black woman, my father was disowned. For marrying a white man, my mother was called a traitor; her racial loyalty and political integrity, inextricable to some, were suddenly subject to indiscriminate cross-examination. Nonetheless, years later, when we are sitting in a living room in San Francisco, far far away from Mississippi, my mother tells me about the hope she and my father had for me, for the world my mixed-race integrated body might help create.

When she talks I listen, floating in an ironic reverie. Given what I know of the seemingly intractable need for human beings to define themselves in relation to a lesser, oppressable Other, it is almost impossible for me to imagine having this kind of faith in the future. But there is a tinge of proud determination in her voice, a rumble of intensely focused righteousness, which I find instructive. My parents believed in a better world because imagining and working toward one was what they did every day.

The young mother and I go at it for a while. I maintain that there is a "real" world to be negotiated, but not wholly defined by. There are parallel worlds, I say, internal and external, no less real. She posits that black people are going to be the only ones who accept her daughter anyway, so why should she set her up for rejection by letting her think she's related to whiteness? It takes all I've got not to scream out, "Because she is, whether they like it or not!" But I don't, and instead I sit calmly, almost missing my plane, glued to an orange wool auditorium seat, fighting on behalf of a child I will probably never meet.

By the time one of the women who will be driving me to the airport finally insists that I leave that very second, I feel narrowly vindicated. The young mother has conceded that irrespective of everything else, the importance of telling the truth, living in truth, knowing the truth, and whatever other truism with the word *truth* in it I can come up with in fifty seconds is extremely important.

As I walk away I tell her about the clerk in Jackson, the boy at Yale, and all of the other people who have questioned the veracity of my existence. People are going to question your daughter no matter what, I say. She may as well be armed and prepared to fight back with what *is,* rather than what those people *wish* was. And besides, I say with a big grin, hoping this young woman doesn't think of me as hopelessly naive and duped by the white male supremacy, "The worst that can happen is that she will end up as confused as me!"

place to rinse before stepping in
lace to rinse before stepping in a plac
o rinse before stepping in a place t
nse before stepping in a place to rins
efore stepping in a place to rinse be
re stepping in a place to rinse befor
epping in a place to rinse before step
ng in a place to rinse before steppin
a place to rinse before stepping in
ace to rinse before stepping in a plac
rinse before stepping in a place t
nse before stepping in a place to rins
efore stepping in a place to rinse be
re stepping in a place to rinse befor
epping in a place to rinse before step
ng in a place to rinse before steppin
a place to rinse before stepping in
ace to rinse before stepping in a plac
rinse before stepping in a place t

U B U D

B ali is this hot, wet, lush, steamy place like none I've ever seen. Everything is green and red and yellow and blue and blooming and it rains heavy hard drops for an hour every afternoon. While I'm here I wear long gauzy skirts and tank tops in muted colors. Flip-flops. I wrap my hair with strips of Kente cloth so that my dreads stick straight up out of the top of my head, and I walk.

I walk to the restaurant surrounded by ponds filled with white lotus blossoms, their thick green stems snaking and entangled beneath the surface of the still water. To the rickety, steaming hot post office to mail the long letters I write to Andrew every day. To the woman who sells silver jewelry and teaches me, every day that I come, a new word in Balinese. To the waterfall I can see from the little porch outside my room across a field of emerald-green rice paddies. To the local artists' collective, two cement rooms covered wall to wall and floor to ceiling with brightly colored oil paintings. To the village shrine, carrying my offering of white blossoms I pick up from the ground along the way.

And I walk to the Monkey Forest at the end of Monkey Forest Road. With my wrinkled brown paper bag filled with peanuts I step tentatively into the dark wood, passing under shards of yellow light that push through treetops far above my head. At first I see nothing, but then I hear rustling and catch some movement out of the corner of my eye. I start to make out forms in the trees and on the ground. When my eyes adjust to the darkness I see dozens of tree monkeys.

En masse they come limping, dragging, swinging, and jumping to get my peanuts. And then I am surrounded by them, tens of furry gray-brown creatures with hands, faces, mouths, and the most expressive eyes I've ever seen. And then I've got monkeys all over me: in my hair, hanging on my arms, standing on the tops of my feet. I feel their solid little bodies, heavy, insistent, and pressing against me, almost knocking me down. Even though I'm no match for them and I've practically got monkey hair between my teeth, I go head to head with their wild willfulness. I hide the peanuts in a secret pocket at the side of my skirt and dole them out one by one to the large and the small, the aggressive and the shy, judiciously placing the rough, dry nuts into tiny, impatient fingers.

When the peanuts have been gobbled, the dry shells forgotten and scattered around our feet, we sit for a while, me and the monkeys, in the dark patch of forest, looking expectantly at one another. I want to keep their attention now that I have no goodies, I want them to stay with me, and so I talk to them. I ask how they're doing and do they like it here in this forest and do the tourists irritate them. Do they eat other things besides peanuts? How many families are they?

We are sitting in a semicircle, me and the monkeys, with me at the center, them all arced around me the way, I guess, monkeys do, like at a council meeting. They don't talk back, but they do watch me with big moist eyes, staring expressively as if to say that talking is absolutely the most pathetic and primitive mode of communication ever. Shut up and sit here! is what they say with their eyes and with the perfect stillness of their bodies. Sit and enjoy the forest and being here together and well, we just ate so sit here with us and enjoy the wonderful feeling we now have, of being full and satisfied.

And so I do.

W alking uphill toward my little room at the other end of the village a few hours later, I am more aware of happenings on the road: the new concrete structures going up, the large squares of bamboo growing on the outskirts of the rice paddies, the intricately carved stone shrines festooned with offerings nestled in the muddy ditches by the side of the road, the women up to their calves in swirling sudsy water washing clothes in the village stream. It is like all my senses have been heightened by sitting stock still in the forest, and now nothing escapes my notice.

A young black man on a motorcycle passes as I walk, turning his head to see the other black person on this road. He grins and waves, waves and grins as we recognize each other as fellow travelers, fellow foreigners, fellow young black people on a road in Bali.

After he passes in something a little slower than a blur, he turns around and after a few minutes we are sitting in the satay shack by the rushing part of the river, sucking fresh banana smoothies through straws.

His name is Christian and he's French Cameroonian and he's just finished doing his military service and because his English is not too good and my French is much worse, I can't tell if the service was for France or Cameroon, but I know that he is beautiful and that I am mesmerized by his glowing dark brown skin and strong sculpted features, by the gap in his perfect white teeth and by the way he says you know in a French patois kind of way after every few words, gesturing with his hands to make his point. He tells me that he was in the service for three years, three years in jail he says, three years wanting to get out and see beauty and not be killing or thinking about killing. He tells me that he almost went crazy there and that's why he's here, on his motorcycle, riding through Indonesia. He says he is trying to get his soul back. To get, "how do you say in English," he says, patting the slight hollow in the center of his chest with the flat of his palm, "my self back."

I listen to Christian, trying to understand all of his words but saying little. There is not a lot to say, to think about, not a lot to make of our meeting. He is a boy traveling, looking for freedom and release. He is very beautiful and sincere. I am a girl on holiday, wandering, opening to this place, to warmth and emptiness. For a short time, maybe an hour, sitting with me is part of his freedom. He is someone to whom I open. We enjoy the space we make.

When Christian rides off on his *moto,* I've got his address and he mine and he tells me he might be back this way in a few days but it might be a few weeks and really I don't think I'll see him again and that's okay and so I'm waving at him and grinning as he chugs off, gathering speed, with a cigarette between his pinkish-brown lips.

I meet Ketut Urip a few days later down at the lotus blossom cafe. He speaks Balinese and I don't and so we make a lot of hand gestures and strange, silly sounds, drawing out vowels in a vain attempt to register meaning. I draw pictures on napkins and Ketut looks at them, nods, and then doesn't draw a response. I guess he is about seventeen, smoking to seem older, cooler than his timid, gentle manner suggests. We eat salad and drink lemonade and then afterward he motions to his motorcycle, lying on its side by the road in front of the lotus ponds.

I hesitate as he rights it, looking around at exactly no one witnessing me or my imminent departure. But I gather my skirt between my legs and climb on the back anyway, liking the feel of the warm black leather between my legs. As he jump-starts the machine I hold on to him so that I don't fall off, grabbing his waist, which is warm and steady. As he rises up and then down, up and then down again trying to get it to start, to get the engine to catch, my cheek rubs against his striped shirt, the bridge of my nose presses into his back. He doesn't seem to notice.

Ketut drives through the village and up a dirt road I am seeing for the first time. To your village? I ask him, screaming into his ear to be heard above the noise of the motor. To your village, he repeats, nodding as if he has understood even though the words aren't right. I try not to notice that this road goes straight up the side of the mountain, and hold on to Ketut tightly as we go over bumps and wind around ducks, chickens, and children who jump out in front of us.

One hour goes by, and then another. As we climb and climb, we pass many villages, a village being four or five gingerly constructed shacks by the side of the road all pressed together. I give up ever being able to get back down the mountain on my own and stifle any thoughts that I may be abducted, never seen or heard from again. I force myself to trust that Ketut has enough gas to get us back, that he's not a Balinesian serial killer, that I can negotiate whatever may happen. Almost there? I scream. Ketut nods, turns the accelerator for more speed, looks determinedly ahead.

I am about to give up and decide I can't take it anymore and to tell Ketut he must turn around and take me back because this is too far and my mother will worry, when we pull up to a clearing in the tall grass that has edged both sides of the road for the last twenty minutes. Ketut steps off the bike, waits patiently for me to follow, puts the kickstand down, and motions for me to follow him down a beaten path. I am hot, sweaty, impatient, uncertain of what will be around the bend.

After a few steps, I hear water, the soft low voices of women talking, and a child splashing. Another step and then I see it, Ketut moving to the side and grinning at me for the first time since we left the restaurant. He has brought me to a gigantic stone bathing temple, I don't know what else to call it. It is a stone vat three times my height, with half-woman half-mermaid winged creatures sprouted from its edges. Clear water gushes out the stone lips of another mythical beast, filling the huge tub over and over again with a rich, bassy gurgle.

Beyond the temple are endless green stepped rice paddies. On the cement steps leading up to it are colorful bits of cloth laid out flat to dry. Oasis, miracle, a more humane culture; I try to name this experience as I slowly approach splashing kids and slips of women gliding around what I can feel now is cool water, prompted by Ketut's firm hand at my back.

Ketut leaves me and goes off to his side, the men's side, and I am alone with a few women a bit older than me, and two baby girls. I want to do everything right and so I smile, bow slightly, and begin to slip off my shoes, unwrap my skirt. I look around for a place to rinse before stepping in. My biggest fear is that I will get in without doing something first, like cleaning off, and that I will contaminate the precious water with my ignorance. But the women are welcoming; they smile at me graciously, giggling at me and my almost ridiculous self-consciousness.

Some time goes by, time in which I float and bathe in what feels like the cleanest, purest river, stare up at a sparkling blue sky and out at the lushest landscape. I feel, literally, as if I am in a dream. When the air starts to cool, Ketut peeks his head around discreetly, keeping his eyes respectfully averted, and motions that he will be waiting for me. I dress and then we travel down the mountain in a kind of spent, relaxed silence. When he drops me off in front of the little house my mother has rented, I thank him and invite him in for tea. He declines. I thank him again, putting my hands to my chest in a prayer and adding a slight bow of my head. He smiles, our eyes meet, and then he turns, rides away, and is gone.

W hen I am in college I travel with my mother and also alone to Greece, England, Ireland, Spain, France, Holland. In Spain people tell me I must be a "dirty Mexican" because I don't speak Spanish with the lisp left over from a stuttering king, and in France I am treated like the Algerian I am presumed on many occasions to be. Waiters ignore me, hotel concierges forget my cleaning or otherwise botch my requests, and cab drivers pass me and my friends on the street without so much as a glance. In England, when I go there with Andrew to visit his relatives in Cornwall, my race is completely unspoken, a subject which is obviously on people's minds but is utterly taboo, as if it represents something beyond words, beyond comprehension. As if not speaking about race except to spit tersely whenever it does come up that it doesn't matter at all is proof that the British are tolerant, progressive, accepting.

But when I am in high school and my mother starts to make more money, we travel to Jamaica, Mexico, Bali. We go as tourists, but because my mother is an artist and makes an effort to meet other artists everywhere we go, and because we are people of color who take the time to learn as much as we can about the culture we are visiting, and because we treat the people we meet as if they are human beings and not objects there solely to respond to our every whim, we are embraced by people, taken in like family.

In these places where many of the people have skin the same color as mine and where I am not embroiled in the indigenous racial politics of the day, I get a glimpse of a kind of freedom I have not experienced at home, where I always seem to be waiting for a bomb to drop and where I feel I am always being reminded of the significance, for better or worse, of my racial inheritance. In the race-obsessed United States, my color defines me, tells a story I have not written. In countries of color I feel that I am defined by my interactions with people. How open I am, how willing to truly see and be seen by another. What skills do I bring? How able am I to communicate, even when we speak a different language?

My lover asks me late one night, when we are all bundled up and close under our comforter and our child has long since gone to be with his grandparents for the summer, what it feels like to have white inside of me. What does it *feel* like to have white inside of you, she asks, and I can hear the burning curiosity in her voice. Physically, you mean? Yeah, physically. Are you aware that there is white in you and does that whiteness feel different from blackness? What is it like to have thin curly hair and lighter skin, what does it *feel* like?

Her question throws me, but only for a few seconds. My first response is, What is whiteness? And how can one "feel white" when race is just about the biggest cultural construct there is? She nods, she's heard me deconstruct it all a million times. Yeah yeah yeah, but if you're operating within it, come on, let yourself go, do you ever *feel* anything different? Well, I say. The only time I "feel white" is when black folks point out something in me that they don't want to own in themselves and so label "white." My tendency to psychoanalyze, for example, or my greater tolerance for cold. My hard-earned sense of entitlement is another example, or my insistence on physical beauty wherever I live, which, ironically, comes from the black side of my family tree.

I also "feel white" when I compare myself physically to darker people and find myself lacking. I most experience whiteness then, as a lack of some attribute or another. A lack of a certain kind of thickness, of a particular full, round, "womanly" shape that I find beautiful and associate with abundance. A lack of color, of the richness, depth, and luminosity that I see in skin darker than my own. A lack of a non-neurotic quality, a kind of freedom from obsessive mental anguish, which I admit I definitely lack, thanks to the Jewish folks in my life.

I don't exactly think to myself, Oh I feel white, at those particular moments, but I do carry a constant sense of not black in those areas, of deprivation in those areas, of wanting to have more of something other than what I have. But is whiteness something I can feel on or in my body like a stomachache or a burn? No.

I ask her if she feels black. Yes is her instant reply. And because her mother was so color conscious, all her life associating goodness with lighter-skinned black people and evil with those darker, and because she went to one of the most color-stratified black colleges in the country and because dark skin is generally reviled in a culture that deifies whiteness, she says she feels an instant kinship with those who are darker, who share her brownness, who have been raised with the same shit hurled at them, the same messages to have to rewrite. She feels black, all of the time.

She says, on the tail end of all that, So like when someone black starts talking about "my people" have been oppressed for so long, do you identify with those people? Do you feel that bond in your gut, can you throw your fist up behind that? Do you think of black people as your people?

I sense we are headed into a danger zone. Is this a test? I breathe. I do and I don't, I say. I was never granted the luxury of being claimed unequivocally by any people or "race" and so when someone starts talking about "my people" I know that if we look hard enough or scratch at the surface long enough, they would have some problem with some part of my background, the part that's not included in the "my people" construction. It's not that I am not loved and accepted by friends and family, it is just that there is always the thing that sets me slightly apart, the "cracker" lurking in my laugh.

And then there is the question of how I can feel fully identified with "my people" when I have other people, too, who are not included in that grouping. And this feeling I have, of having other people too, is in effect even when the other people under consideration do not claim me. Does that make sense? I ask. She nods.

What I do feel is an instant affinity with beings who suffer, whether they are my own, whatever that means, or not. Do I identify with the legacy of slavery and discrimination in this country? Yes. Do I identify with the legacy of anti-Jewish sentiment and exclusion? Yes. Do I identify with the internment of Japanese-

Americans during World War Two? Yes. Do I identify with the struggle against brutality and genocide waged against the Native Americans in this country? Yes. Do I feel I have to choose one of these allegiances in order to know who I am or in order to pay proper respect to my ancestors? No. Do I hope that what my ancestors love in me is my ability to muster compassion for those who suffer, including myself? Yes.

It seems to me that this, too, is how memory works. What we remember of what was done to us shapes our view, molds us, sets our stance. But what we remember is past, it no longer exists, and yet still we hold on to it, live by it, surrender so much control to it. What do we become when we put down the scripts written by history and memory, when each person before us can be seen free of the cultural or personal narrative we've inherited or devised?

When we, ourselves, can taste that freedom?

so I changed my name so I changed my name so I changed my name so I change my name so I changed my name so I changed my name so I changed my name so I changed my name so I changed m name so I changed my name so I change my name so I changed my name so I changed my name so I changed my name so I changed m name so I changed my name so I change my name so I changed my name so I changed my name so I changed my name so I changed m name so I changed my name so I change my name so I changed my name so I changed my name so I changed my name so I changed m name I changed my name so I change my name I changed my name so

In twelfth grade I am at the height of my power as a young woman. I am experienced. I am loved. I am excelling in my classes. I am president of my school and lead all school meetings in the gym every week. I write essays that are published in the school paper. I help develop programs that will raise awareness of people of color at my school. I drive. I apply to college. I go to Muir Beach with the white upper-class classmates I have felt estranged from for three years and drink beer in a borrowed beach house without wanting to kill them or myself in the process.

Over the past three years I have evolved into a full-fledged progressive, politicized Bay Area person. I have dreadlocks down to my shoulders that I wear wrapped in multicolored strips of cloth from Guatemala. I wear long dangling earrings made by Native Americans. And above my desk hang a black-and-white poster of a glowing young woman holding a rifle in one hand and a nursing baby in the other, and a set of photographs of an enormous Buddha being ceremonially washed and adorned with flowers.

This year Bob Marley is my favorite musician, and along with books by William Faulkner and Flannery O'Connor that I read for school, I devour the work of Frantz Fanon, Mahatma Gandhi, June Jordan, Angela Davis, and Andrea Dworkin. I believe that if I am not part of the solution I am part of the problem, and I am determined to be on the right side of any and all equations having to do with social justice.

So I change my name.

In twelfth grade I decide to move Leventhal to the more obscure middle position in my name and add Walker to the end, privileging my blackness and downplaying what I think of as my whiteness. After all, why should my father get all of the credit? Why should that line, that clan of people who have been so resistant to my birth, be allowed to claim the young woman I have become?

This comes as a shock to my father and stepmother, but in my mother's house the shift feels completely normal, expected even. My mother and I have talked about giving me a different name for years, she pushing for more inclusion, more matrilineal bonding, and me open to it. What about Walkingtall, she might call out from the kitchen. Or Levenwalk. I nod, grin, imagine it. I want to be closer to my mother, to have something run between us that cannot be denied. I want a marker that links us tangibly and forever as mother and daughter. That links me tangibly and forever with blackness.

A few days after my seventeenth birthday I drive myself down to the city courthouse and fill out a dozen forms in triplicate, writing in Rebecca Grant Leventhal as the name I no longer want, and Rebecca Leventhal Walker as the name I choose. I shuffle from line to line until finally I stand before a judge who asks me why, if I am not marrying or divorcing, I am giving up my father's name, my given name. I tell him all that is required, that I have personal reasons, and then he orders my mother or legal guardian to appear before he will allow it.

I wait until it is all done, and my mother has come back from court with ten copies of the stamped and sealed official form declaring my new name, to call my father. He is quiet for a few moments after I tell him, sitting at the center of an angry silence. When he does speak, he suggests that my choice has something to do with my own anti-Semitism, with wanting to distance myself from the Jewish in me. When he says that, questioning my motivations, oblivious to my reality, I feel like I have been hit in the stomach, betrayed in the deepest place. I react defensively, asking why I should want the name of the man who disowned my father when he was only eight years old. Why I should carry the name of the man who beat my grandmother and has refused to this day to see me or any other of his son's children.

But it is more than that, so much more that I can't bring myself to explain to my father. When I change my name I do so because I do not feel an affinity with whiteness, with what Jewishness has become, and I do feel an affinity with blackness, with an experience of living in the world with non-white skin. While my black friends are shuttled through mediocre schools into poorly paid jobs in the service industry and I escape only by the grace of God, my father has seemingly stopped caring about all things racial and political and has settled into a comfortable routine commuting from Westchester and going to lily-white Little League games in pristine suburban ballparks. I do not see how I fit into his life, or that I want to.

MOVEMENT CHILD

·

W hen the school year ends and my father comes to San Francisco for my graduation it is the first time since the divorce that I see my parents together in a non-public place, and it is the first time that I have to negotiate feeling that I must be visibly and emotionally loyal to both of them at the same time. This means trying to draw my father out and obediently making tea and responding to my mother's every request. It means worrying that my father will not feel comfortable in what is clearly "black space," home space that has not included him and from which he and all signs relating to the life he leads back in New York are absent. It means praying my mother doesn't mention the Palestinians and my father doesn't talk about Israel. I am so nervous, I barely think about my graduation. I am supposed to be writing and polishing up my speech, but I cannot take my mind off these two grown-ups who to me, with my irrational need to protect each from the other, seem more like children.

The day before the ceremony, my parents are careful and each guarded, both of them skating across the surface without submerging any part, studiously avoiding waters they might lack the skills to navigate. My father sits in our living room like a stranger, barely looking beyond his teacup, and asks banal questions about the rainy season, my mother's siblings, and the new biography of Martin Luther King, Jr. My mother sits in a rocking chair, shelling pecans and offering uncharacteristically terse replies.

As they sit, leaden and stiff in their respective corners, I cannot. Every seat I choose seems too close to one of them, and I jump up for fear I might be perceived as taking one side over the other. Instead I flit around the living room trying to build a bridge of memory between them. I ask question after question, hoping to jog their collective memory of the time I was born and we lived our life together as a family. When sitting together, making sense as a group and as an idea, was what we did all the time. They all but ignore me. My father laughs nervously when I ask about Jackson, about how they met, my mother waves her hand in front of her face and asks about the time. Hadn't we better get going?

In a photograph taken on graduation day I beam out from the center of my hodgepodge family, dressed all in white and carrying an armful of calla lilies. My mother stands to my right, looking cold and uncomfortable, Robert and Andrew stand on my left, oblivious and proud. My father looks pained and displaced, standing ramrod straight at the edge of our little group, his face mostly covered by dark sunglasses.

I want to remember a day filled with tearful goodbyes to my

classmates and heartfelt hugs from my teachers who gave me so much and believed in me so deeply, but all I can remember is my father sticking his rib cage out to look less hunched over and my mother remote and distant, pulled back into a charade of total composure and control. I remember that I felt myself to be the only link between them, because only I could see the quivering vulnerability lying just below both of their careful presentations, and only I wanted desperately to make it all okay.

START AGAIN

Watching TV, I catch glimpses of the future, shimmering moments which embody shifts of consciousness on a monumental scale. Last night two documentaries: one on the life of Pearl Buck and the other on Nelson Mandela and his struggle to, as one of his ANC comrades put it, "liberate blacks from bondage and whites from fear." The intimate details of Pearl Buck's life were offered by her numerous and varied-in-hue children. The one who moved me was relatively young, articulate, and warm, with glowing brown skin and sad, darker brown eyes. She spoke devotedly of her mother: Buck's dislike of fame and love of travel, her regimented relationships and her failed attempts at writing plays. As this brown daughter spoke, the filmmakers cut to various images of Buck, the palest of white women with the stiffest and most formal manner of all those in her presence.

In the special on Mandela we see the prisons that held him for thirty years, the South African police shooting into crowds of singing children. We see minutes from secret meetings suggesting the release of Mandela, but only if he is so physically compromised he cannot function. And then we hear of Mandela meeting with Botha, see Mandela shaking the hand of de Klerk, and we cannot imagine how difficult this handshake must have been. At the end of the documentary, Mandela convenes a group of women: wives of the white Afrikaaner leaders, black South African women leaders, and wives of ANC leaders. Colorful, zaftig, hearty, this group of twenty sit at a long oval table, pouring and drinking tea. Mandela hosts in a trademark dress shirt, showing an awkward Mrs. Botha to her chair, working in his subtle way to keep everything at the right pitch. To his right, a black woman in a purple headdress smiles knowingly as she tilts her head and listens to what Mrs. de Klerk has to say.

These women don't clasp hands and skip off into the setting sun, but they do sit with one another in the same room drinking from the same teapot, recognizing each other if not as equals then at least as fellow human beings. This, no matter how frightening the blacks seem to the whites in the rightness of their cause. This, no matter how barbaric the whites seem to the blacks in their maniacal defense of thievery.

I fantasize that my father and I create similar glimpses of a more expansive consciousness. As we walk down the street arm in arm and engage in deep father-daughter talk at our favorite Chinese restaurant, we come together not as guilty and wronged but as two in love and in struggle with each other, each searching to know and understand the other's truth. I often think that our blood tie is critical, the thread which forces us to stay connected, but I also believe that blood ties are less important, that all blood

BLACK, WHITE, AND JEWISH

is basically the same, that I am just as protective of my adopted son with whom I share not a drop as I am of the sister who shares with me my father's eyes and our grandfather's jaw.

When my grandmother finally dies, slipping from dementia to coma straight into some other world I can only imagine from here, I know it is mainly experience which binds us, memory, and not blood. Now, only I hold the memories of our time together. Only I nurture our relationship, massaging it to yield sustenance, a sense of being connected through time and space and culture. My brother and sister, also my grandmother's grandchildren, do not feel as I do. The blood is as thick but the investment is not.

At my grandmother's grave, my father stands watching the men shovel earth over her coffin. I rub his back, trying to imagine burying my mother, my father, my pillars, the ones I know like a part of my own body even though there are so many secrets. I imagine my grandmother's tiny, cold body as I have seen it that morning, squeezed into the pine box with the Jewish star on top. It all comes to this, my father says with tears in his eyes, turning away. It all comes to this.

My grandmother sat shiva as if my father had died when my parents married, and then twenty years later introduced me with her chest poked out to whoever would listen. She was stubborn, generous, desperately lonely. What is left of that life lived? My memories perhaps, the imprint she left on the being that is me that goes on after all this, the effects passed on nameless to my children and their children, biological and not.

It all comes to this. I stand with those who stand with me. I am tired of claiming for claiming's sake, hiding behind masks of culture, creed, religion. My blood is made from water and so it is bloodwater that I am made of, and so it is a constant empathic link with others which claims me, not only carefully drawn lines of relation. I exist somewhere between black and white, family and friend. I am flesh and blood, yes, but I am also ether.

This, too, is how memory works.

ACKNOWLEDGMENTS

My gratitude to all of the people who touched my life, some of whose names and identifying characteristics I had to change in order to protect their privacy and publish this book. I am also deeply indebted to the Macdowell Colony, the Corporation of Yaddo, Adolfo Profumo, Wendy Weil, Sheryl Nields, and the visionary women at Riverhead Books, especially my editor, Amy Hertz.

The last words of this book I extend to my family and friends, alive and dead, biological and not. Gratitude to Adrienne, Askia, Bashir, Ben, Benedetto, Celina, Dereje, Gregoriah, Imani, Jessica, Julia, Karla G., Katie, Kevin, Kofi, Marcus John, Meri, Paul, Pratibha, Shaheen, and especially Trajal. Thank you. Without you I could not be.

ABOUT THE AUTHOR

Rebecca Walker was educated at Yale University, and her work has appeared in numerous anthologies and publications including *Harper's, Ms.,* the *Utne Reader, Vibe,* and *Spin.* She has hosted television forums and produced segments for national and public television, and is a founder of Third Wave Foundation, the only national activist philanthropic organization for young women between the ages of fifteen and thirty. Walker has lived most recently in New York City and now resides in northern California.